SOUL OF AN ATHLETE

STORIES AND LESSONS ON LIFE POST-ATHLETICS

D1606686

FROM FORMER ELITE ATHLETES
ATHLETES SOUL INC.
& CONTRIBUTING AUTHORS

WWW.SELFPUBLISHN30DAYS.COM

Published by *Self Publish -N- 30 Days*

© Copyright 2023 Athletes Soul Inc.

Printed in the United States of America
ISBN: 979-8-85314-193-3
1. Self-help 2. Athletics 3. Personal Growth
Athletes Soul Inc., *Soul of An Athlete*
Disclaimer/Warning:

This book is intended for lecture and informative purposes only. This publication is designed to provide competent and reliable information regarding the subject matter covered. The author or publisher is not engaged in rendering legal or professional advice. Laws vary from state to state, and if legal, financial, or other expert assistance is needed, the services of a professional should be sought. The author and publisher disclaim any liability incurred from the use or application of the contents of this book.

TABLE OF CONTENTS

INTRODUCTION

For many athletes, the sport that they compete in defines their life. They dedicate countless hours, years, and even decades of their lives to mastering their craft, aiming to reach the pinnacle of their sport. But what happens when that journey comes to an end? What happens when athletes are forced to retire from the sport they have poured so much into?

The question, "Who am I if I am no longer an athlete?" is one that many athletes dread. It is a question that few athletes dare to say out loud before their athletic career ends. There is a widely held belief in the world of sports that thinking about your next career is a sign that your current one is already fading.

"Keep your head in the game."
"Don't be distracted."
"Stay focused on your sport."

These familiar comments from coaches and sometimes family members only reinforce this message. You mustn't think about anything else but your sport, and you shouldn't think about what happens if you don't make it.

However, the pursuit of athletic excellence can have a profound impact on an athlete's emotional development. During adolescence, when other teenagers experiment and develop their own identities, values, and character, athletes singularly focus on mastering their craft.

This dedication drives their performance and success but also transforms them at a deeper level. The significance of this emotional journey is evident when, long after their competitive career is over, athletes continue to introduce themselves as former athletes.

Retirement from athletics is an unavoidable event. All athletes will eventually retire, whether they want it or not. According to a study by Game Plan, only three in ten student-athletes get to choose when to retire from sports. Most will leave their sport due to injury, deselection, the end of their collegiate career, or the lack of playing opportunities. Not all athletes will face an identity crisis, but all will wrestle with identity and self-worth questions.

To address these challenges, a book has been written that explores the stories of fourteen former athletes from ten different sports. Through their personal experiences and reflections, readers can gain insight into the emotional impact of athletic retirement. The book also includes contributions from psychologists and professional coaches who offer advice on the transition process and share what they have learned from working with retiring athletes.

The book is for athletes, coaches, parents, and anyone else who works with or supports athletes. It provides valuable insights into what athletes may be experiencing and how to better support them through retirement. Pursuing excellence in sports can be a lonely and challenging journey, filled with many setbacks and failures, and the end of an athletic career is no different. This book is an excellent resource to help navigate the complex emotional terrain of retiring from athletics.

In addition to emotional challenges, retiring from athletics can bring about practical challenges, such as finding a new career or developing new hobbies and interests. It can be difficult to adjust to a life without the structure and routine that comes with training and competing, and the sudden loss of identity that comes with no longer being a "competitor." But with the right support, athletes can learn to navigate these challenges and find fulfillment in new ways.

Ultimately, the journey of retirement from athletics is a personal one. While there are everyday experiences that many athletes share, each individual will face their own unique challenges and opportunities.

By sharing the stories and insights of retired athletes and the guidance of experts in the field, this book provides a roadmap for navigating this challenging transition. It is a valuable resource for anyone grappling with the question, "Who am I if I am no longer an athlete?" and seeking support in this journey.

PART I

STORIES OF ATHLETIC RETIREMENT

CHAPTER 1

STRIVING HIGHER

BY STEVE DAVIS JR.

When I was young, I never thought football would take me so far. In fact, as a young kid who was involved in many sports, I aspired to play professional baseball or basketball (if I kept growing). However, it wasn't until high school that I realized football would be my ticket to prosperity and a part of my identity for the rest of my life.

Before then, I had only played football once, at the age of nine, and even though I won the MVP award that year, I quit the next year because I didn't feel like it was for me. My teammates and family tried to convince me to stick with it, but I didn't feel the urge to play again until I was about to go to high school.

All my friends I went to school with at that time doubted I was even good at football. They kept saying I was too soft and too nice of a guy to be good on the field. But, you see, I have always been a smart, fun-loving, and respectful guy. So much so that when you get to truly know me, you start to question whether I am the same guy my teammates called "Big Hurt," who was blasting folks on the football field.

But like most elite athletes, I had to find and maintain an edge. Mine was striving to always be great at anything I do, and if anybody doubted me, I'd fight like hell to prove them wrong.

Hearing my peers say I wasn't good enough was all the motivation I needed to go to high school and pour everything into football. After playing on the varsity team during my sophomore year, I gave up my first love of baseball to focus on football.

What I didn't realize going into my new focus on football was the attention and respect I would get from everyone, the skills and lessons I would learn, the doors that would open up, and the love and addiction I would grow for the game. So, while I felt I had an identity outside of sports, I gravitated toward the persona I developed through football.

I had a dominating high school career that brought many accolades and scholarship opportunities to play football at the Division 1 level. By the end of high school, I was touted as the number one prospect in St. Louis, so the chances of making it to the NFL seemed pretty high.

I felt the need to continue playing and live up to the high expectations my city, family, and friends now had for me.

I chose to attend the University of Minnesota because I felt they believed in my ability to play defensive end, the position I was great at but undersized for. They also had a disdain for the Universities of Iowa and Wisconsin. Both basically told me I wasn't good enough to play on their team (remember that edge I talked about?). Believe it or not, I felt like Minnesota provided me with far more opportunities to have a career outside of sports as well. Yes, while going all in on football, I still didn't lose sight of who I was before football took over.

After my freshman year, I felt everything was going according to plan. I became the starter from game one over many seniors and juniors, earning Freshman All-American and All-Big Ten honors. I stuck it to schools that thought I wasn't good enough, and the NFL scouts were drooling over my potential.

My sophomore year saw a slight drop-off from the success of my freshman season, but I was motivated to bounce back and dominate my last two years. A new coaching staff was hired, and I decided to move to a different position to better align with the new coach's philosophy. I thought it would enhance my chances of making it to the NFL in a position more applicable to my size. I showcased my skills, versatility, intelligence, and leadership even more, closing out what I believed was a solid collegiate career.

By this time, you couldn't tell me I wouldn't make it. We had presenters come and talk to our team from time to time to try and open our eyes to other possibilities outside of football, but I wasn't listening. They would always say, "Only three percent of all college athletes will make it to the pros," I would brush it off and think, "Well, I'm in that three percent, so I ain't worried about that." There are thirty-two teams and over two hundred fifty players drafted every year, and I felt I proved to be in the top two hundred, if not one hundred, in the world.

I put on a great showing at my Pro Day and was ready for the opportunity to be drafted. I will never forget what happened next.

My agent indicated he believed I would hear my name called during the draft, so I informed my family. Of course, they were ecstatic. Against my wishes, my family decided to host an NFL Draft watch party with all my friends and family back in St. Louis.

This would be the moment to show everyone I made it and fulfilled the dream. All the hard work and dedication I had put into the game would pay off that day. All the naysayers who didn't think I was good enough would now have to see me on the biggest stage in the world. I decided to go along with it.

Interestingly enough, sitting and watching the draft and waiting to hear my name called was one of the most nerve-wracking experiences of my life—especially with so many people watching me. Any slight buzz of the phone set me off. I couldn't focus on any of the conversations I was having. I could barely taste the food I ate. It almost felt like an out-of-body experience.

I sat there on the couch for what felt like twenty years, waiting to hear my name called. As family and friends enjoyed the party, I stayed glued to the TV and my phone. When the draft ended, and I didn't hear my name called, I immediately went outside and called my agent, searching for some good news.

"Something has to be wrong; there is no way I didn't get drafted, right? At least tell me I'm invited to camp to try out. All I need is a shot, and I will show them all."

My agent told me he would be in touch and believed he could get me a tryout. So, I had to wait and deflect all the questions my family and friends were asking me. At that point, I wanted to run away and hide in shame, but I stayed for the remainder of the party and told everyone to keep hope alive and that it would all work out.

My agent and I traded calls the next few weeks, but nothing substantial was happening. I was becoming more and more fearful that my dream wasn't going to be fulfilled. Out of frustration, I fired my agent, hired a new one, and sent out my tapes to teams on my own. My new agent tried to convince me to think about other football routes to the NFL, like the Arena League, but I was too stubborn and steadfast to listen. To me, it was the NFL or nothing.

After six months of effort, I made one of the most challenging decisions of my life and decided to move on from football. The frustration, embarrassment, and disappointment I felt for myself, and from what I perceived others felt, came rushing through my body in a mountain of tears.

Until then, my identity as a football player dominated my life so much that I had no idea who I was or where I was going next. In my ignorant state of mind, I thought I had control over when my football career would end. I had pictured the ideal pathway that would afford me many opportunities to set me up for life, and in my imagination, it had damn sure never looked like this.

Letting go of my football career was the most humbling experience of my life. From it, I made the brave decision to pick myself up, move to a different state, and start fresh. Staying in St. Louis or going back to Minnesota was too upsetting for me at the time. Even though I could have had some clear opportunities available to me in both cities, I was too prideful and bitter that I didn't want to be in either place.

I was determined to figure out who I truly was on my own. I don't take this part for granted because it is not easy to take that first step after feeling like you lost a part of your soul. I could have easily sat there in my depression for a long time, but there was always a part of me preparing for life outside of football. So why not go out and try? Maybe it is the "show me" and "prove them wrong" mindset I developed in St. Louis, but I have always had a bias toward action.

I received my degree in Mass Communications with a focus on Graphic Design and ideally wanted to find a role working with design. However, I graduated during the 2009 recession, so finding a job without work experience that I couldn't gain while playing football was even harder.

Because of that, I was willing to take almost any job that looked appealing. So, I reached out to my fraternity brothers. They helped me line up an opportunity in Atlanta to interview with Target for an Executive Team Leader position and potentially start my life outside of sports.

Until this point, I had never had a real job interview, but I made it through four rounds and felt pretty confident I would get the job. When they reached out and told me that I didn't get it, it became an additional blow to me and my ego.

Here I was, once the "Golden Child" who always had things work out for me, now without a dollar to my name, no job, sleeping on my frat brother's couch, and no idea what to do next.

If you had told me in high school that I would have ended up like this, I would have laughed at you.

I applied for many jobs and didn't get any of them. It was as if they didn't care that I was *almost* an NFL player. I was clinging so much to my skill set from football that I failed to show who I was outside of sports.

But I was learning.

What changed for me was getting connected with a former player from the University of Minnesota, who owned a company. We sat and talked a little about football and a lot about life. He gave me some great advice that I still use today, and he gave me my first job. I will forever be indebted to him because he helped pull me out of a bad state of mind.

I became a merchandiser for his beer distribution company, and I would wake up early in the mornings to put beer on store shelves. This wasn't a glorious job by any means, and I had to humble myself again and work on the same level as people who didn't even have a high school diploma, but it was an opportunity to work, grow, and learn.

One thing I learned about myself that helped me enjoy each day was paying attention to the aspects of work and life that brought me joy. I tried to do more of that while also keeping note of things I didn't like. This observation helped me navigate many obstacles that arose later in my career.

I also realized the power of connections. I eventually left the beer distribution job because it wasn't what I truly wanted to do or where I felt I was fulfilling my purpose. I reconnected with another alumnus and got a different job (notice a theme?).

This time, I started networking and volunteering while working full-time in areas and groups of interest. When I was playing football, I knew what I wanted to be. Now, I was just trying things, hoping to find what I wanted to do. As I searched, I leveraged people I had developed relationships with to help me.

I did eventually get into some design work, but that wasn't enough for me, so I kept trying other roles. To summarize my job experience, I did some freelance work, worked in sales and marketing, became a project manager, hosted events, volunteered with nonprofits, volunteered as a youth football coach, went to many networking socials, and became a part of a small start-up company devoted to sports and technology.

Hard work is part of the DNA of any athlete, and I decided to channel that hard work into many areas as part of my discovery. I felt I wouldn't know whether I liked something until I experienced it.

Eventually, I noticed a common thread with my experiences. There were former athletes and alumni involved in most of the success in my career, and almost all of them had trouble adjusting to life after athletics. I decided to focus my energy, experience, and skill set on helping others transition.

I stumbled upon an opportunity to return to the University of Minnesota and work at the Alumni Association to become a connector for alumni. My passion and purpose felt aligned for the first time, and everything I learned through my journey was being used positively to help alumni.

It was here that I discovered how much I could impact others and uncovered the philosophy of life I had been using without realizing it. The philosophy is called "Designing Your Life," and it was developed by two Stanford professors, Bill Burnett, and Dave Evans.

It is a "design thinking" framework for life that is built on experimenting and analyzing where you are today and where you want to go. I mentioned my bias towards action before, and Designing Your Life is all about that and building your way forward. It is all about identifying a direction, taking action, and then pausing to reflect and assess.

Failure is embraced and often leads to great outcomes. As athletes, we all fail and are taught to get back up and try again. Life is no different, and perseverance will carry you through many obstacles if you frame them right.

I believe wholeheartedly in the "Designing Your Life" philosophy based on my own experiences and other people's stories. My belief runs so deep that I am striving towards building a life-coaching framework using "Designing Your Life" to help athletes transition. I plan to share more details of my journey, but more importantly, coach other athletes to design and activate their own joyful life after sports as I have.

My life to this point has been a journey of learning, and I encourage you to look at your life in the same way. Even if you accomplish your goals through sports, it will eventually end, and you will have to move on. Be unafraid of failure because there are lessons throughout the highs and lows you experience. Just as we learned to practice in order to improve our ability in our chosen sport, you will have to practice and commit to getting better at facing challenges.

So, keep that same energy in life—and Strive Higher!

ABOUT STEVE

Steve Davis Jr. is a servant leader, design thinker, VP of Engagement, and an athlete transition coach currently residing in Minneapolis, Minnesota. He played four years of football at the University of Minnesota, where he received his B.A. in Mass Communications in 2008.

Steve currently works at the University of Minnesota Alumni Association as the Associate Vice President of Engagement. In this role, he helps oversee engagement for over 500,000 alumni around the world, keeping them connected to the University and each other.

Throughout his career, he has developed extensive experience in creative marketing, communications, and event planning. He has done everything from coaching to strategic planning to creative design to digital communication to project management, all with a design thinking approach. His experience as an athlete and in life has driven him to knock down barriers of access and create bridges of connectivity to help enhance lives and generate a sense of pride.

His moniker for life is "Strive Higher Every Day (S.H.E.D.)," and he lives that out by continuing to be a lifelong learner and inspiring others to do the same.

Steve and his wife, Rikita, have two children: Trevan (TJ) and Rylee.

Connect with Steve:
Instagram: @SHED_AVE
Twitter: @SHED_AVE
LinkedIn: https://www.linkedin.com/in/stevedav/
www.SHEDAvenue.com

CHAPTER 2

FINDING MY SPORT BY ACCIDENT

BY MYRIAM GLEZ

G rowing up in Lyon, France, my family and I loved spending time in the mountains. Whenever we got the chance, we would make the trip to my grandmother's house in the Alps. It was there that I first discovered my love for skiing and hiking.

My parents weren't what I would call athletic; however, my mother thought putting me in tennis when I was young would be a good idea. It quickly became apparent that I had no interest in that sport. I was more interested in cycling around the neighborhood, running through the cornfields, and going to the local pool with my friends.

Whenever I was forced to attend tennis class, I would cause trouble by talking too much or doing pirouettes in the middle of the court. At the end of the season, the tennis coach diplomatically suggested that it might be better for me to try another sport.

Around the same time, I watched Muriel Hermine, the best French synchronized swimmer, compete in the European Championship and win the first medal ever for France. I was captivated by her performance and fell in love with the sport. I remember turning to my mom and saying, "This is what I want to do!" It was a sudden and unexpected declaration, considering I didn't know much about synchronized swimming, but I was determined to give it a try.

I begged my parents to take me to a tryout, but the local club wasn't exactly close to our home. After several months of pestering, my mother finally relented, and I had my chance to impress the coach. The pool was deep and dark, and the coach seemed slightly intimidating, but I was determined to make a good impression.

I swam a lap of freestyle, holding my breath the entire time because I didn't know how to turn my head to take a breath. Surprisingly, the coach was impressed with my technique and offered me a spot on the team.

Synchronized swimming was an unusual choice for me, especially since my parents weren't swimmers. We rarely went on beach holidays, but I learned to swim when I was just three years old. It all started during one of our mountain vacations when we went pedal boating with my uncle and cousins.

In the middle of the lake, the boat started taking on water and quickly sank. I remember the water being green and drinking water between breaths, but my uncle saved my cousin and me by carrying us to shore.

Looking back, that moment in the lake might have been the beginning of my love for swimming. Instead, it led me to synchronized swimming, a sport that I fell in love with at first sight. It's funny how life works out sometimes - if that boat had never sunk, I might have never discovered my passion for synchronized swimming.

After that episode, my parents put me in swimming lessons, and I discovered a love for the water. Each summer, I would stay a month at my auntie's house and spend the entire day in their pool.

From morning to night, I played in the water until my skin was soft and tanned, and my hair was turning green from the chemicals in the pool! Because my mom was still afraid of me drowning, I continued taking summer swim lessons until I perfected all strokes. Practicing a water sport all year was a good way to extend my summer holidays!

Early days – seeds for a dream

I have very few memories of my early days in the sport because I started so early–at six years old. What I remember is more of an overall feeling: the excitement of going to the pool, having fun with my friends, learning new skills, creating routines, and the satisfaction of physical exhaustion after a good practice. I progressed quickly, training every day of the week. The sport absorbed my energy and attention.

My training quickly became a logistical challenge as I moved to middle school because my school was so far away from the pool. I had to take the local bus, the subway, and another city bus. The whole journey would take an hour and a half every day.

Most days, I would run to the bus stop after classes, carrying my training bag and my school bag full of books. I tried to sit as close to the front of the bus as possible to do my homework without too many road bumps.

Now with perspective, I realize how much of a commitment this was. Not only was it physically demanding, especially in the winter when it was frigid, but it required a lot of trust from my parents to let me travel by myself at 11 years old throughout the countryside and the city. This forced me to be mature early on, punctual, independent, responsible, and aware of my surroundings.

During that time, I started mentioning to people that I wanted to go to the Olympics. Like other kids, I watched the games on television and enjoyed following the national team athletes. I was devastated when Muriel Hermine missed the podium in the Olympics in Seoul in 1988 but vowed to be there myself at some point. There were no national or international level athletes in my club. I now realize how unrealistic my goal would have seemed to my coaches and teammates at the time.

Competing – committing to my goal

I was a stubborn and motivated kid. My parents knew better than to discourage me from pursuing my goals. I was set on competing for the national team in the Olympics. From twelve years old onwards, I did everything possible to achieve that goal. That meant training six days per week during school vacations and the summer holidays.

It also meant attending a different school to be closer to the pool and to have a more flexible school schedule. This was a big financial commitment for my family, as only private schools offered this type of flexibility back then. It also required reorganization of the family schedule, with my dad driving me to the school each morning, a 45-minute to one-hour drive, followed by public transportation (subway, bus, and walking) in the afternoons to go to practice. The flexible hours, understanding teachers, and other student-athletes made everything worthwhile.

I never questioned the worth of my commitment or if I would achieve my goal. Because of that, it never seemed like a burden. What others often saw as a sacrifice, I saw as an opportunity. I didn't mind missing out on "normal school" experiences or socializing with friends. Instead, I focused on the things I was able to do as a young athlete: meet incredible people and travel throughout my country and the world.

I also discovered and challenged myself in ways that were uncommon for kids my age. This isn't talked about much, but it's an incredible opportunity for a young person to have the space to discover what they are made of!

Not everybody is able to find and dive into a single passion early on in life. However, this process of bettering yourself in a specific field yields significant personal lessons. While these aren't obvious at that age, they will be foundational and beneficial at any stage of life.

While my non-athlete friends spent time together, I trained, competed, and traveled. I was already on a different path. I didn't spend time with them after school, shopping, or going to the movies.

By thirteen, I had traveled all over the country and overseas for training camps and competitions. I met athletes from different teams in France and in Europe. I'd faced challenging competitions where I'd failed, but I had also won several national titles and participated in the Youth National Teams.

My elite sporting journey – commitment, resilience, and hard work!

One summer, I received a letter from the French Swimming Federation inviting me to relocate to the National Training Center in Paris. I was fourteen. I was over the moon. The National Training Center is where all top Olympians train. In Synchronized Swimming, only a handful of athletes get invited, carefully selected by the National Team coach. This was a once-in-a-lifetime opportunity that, as an athlete, you couldn't really pass on.

This invitation meant moving five hours from home to a campus similar to that of a big university with all facilities - athletics, academics, and living quarters—all grouped in one location. This also meant I would have to live on my own.

I never even considered not going! I was so driven and focused on my goal that this wasn't an option. I knew I had to be at the National Training Center to have a chance of being selected for the Olympics.

The transition was harder than I expected. I liked the independence and the ability to train with the best athletes. I didn't mind leaving my school and friends behind. I had a clear direction, and I would have done anything to achieve that goal. Leaving my hometown was a necessary step.

I couldn't wait to meet other athletes with the same goals

as me. I often felt disconnected from kids my age who weren't athletes. I felt they didn't understand my lifestyle choices and why I was never available to spend time with them.

The new training pace was brutal. I went from three hours of daily training to six or seven. At my club, I was the best, but suddenly, I had to work hard to be able to follow the older athletes. For the first six months, I was constantly tired and hungry! In addition, I had to learn to live independently, stay on top of my studies, and plan my travels back home to visit family. It was a lot of learning all at once, and it definitely took me a while to find my pace and balance.

Despite, or thanks to, these challenges, this was a period of immense growth for me. In this environment, as a 14-year-old, you could easily lose yourself. I had a lot of freedom, which could have led to poor choices.

Many of my teammates and other athletes either partied too much, which affected their athletic performances, or didn't study and were completely absorbed by their sport. The first few months at the training center were definitely testing. I fell into that trap. I experimented and engaged in social life and partied with older athletes.

Surprisingly, I think my biggest challenge was food. I was training so much that I was constantly hungry. For the first time, I had to choose what to eat and how much. The cafeteria offered an unlimited amount of food, and I never felt full enough.

After the first six months, I had put on 10 kilos. In an artistic sport like synchronized swimming, this is a big hindrance. I felt heavier in the pool and much more body conscious. I felt ashamed the first time I went back home to my family and teammates.

After some trial and error, I re-centered on what was most important to me: my studies and my sport. I became more conscious of the importance of my daily choices and how they affected my practice and progression. Being able to know early on what your values are and why you are choosing that particular path is really important. It obviously supported my athletic and academic performance, but it also allowed me to view what others considered sacrifices as opportunities.

The several years I spent at the National Training Center were certainly not straightforward. Like any athlete, I faced some challenges. I had several injuries. I had to learn how to handle the coaching structure and decisions.

I had to assert myself in a team of mostly older, more experienced athletes. I made mistakes at competitions and didn't always get the desired results. Dealing with these road bumps forced me to rethink my approach, honestly analyze my skills, and learn to self-advocate for my position to the coaches. Every few months, I seemed to face a new difficulty that would lead to self-reflection, a different response, and an opportunity for personal development.

Difficult choice – looking forward

Over a period of seven or eight years, I traveled extensively to international competitions. I participated in multiple European, World, and Olympic competitions while pursuing my academic journey.

Although I made many decisions to pursue my sport dream, my education was always important to me. I was a very good student and wanted to attend a top university or school. I put a lot of effort into my high school studies to create the best opportunity possible for my secondary studies.

There are no collegiate sports in France, so you have to plan your studies around your sport. I ended up starting a bachelor's degree after high school, deferring one year to prepare for the Olympics in Sydney, and resuming my degree after the Games to transfer to a top school. This was a challenging time, as I was one of the few athletes to continue her education after high school while being on the team.

I was often in conflict with my coaches on the topic. They would complain about me having to take time off from practice for my exams and would threaten to take me off the roster.

In the middle of my second Olympic campaign, and after an intense summer of studying, I got accepted into one of the top business schools in France. This was an incredible moment for me! I received that news while competing at the World Cup in Zurich. And whilst I was over the moon about achieving that goal, I was also confused and disappointed in my coaches. Following that news, the coaching staff seemed upset and stopped talking to me. The rest of the competition felt like a blur while I struggled with loneliness and mixed feelings.

A few weeks after the competition, I was asked by the National Team coaches to a meeting where they asked me to choose between attending business school and pursuing my Olympic campaign. This came as a complete shock. I didn't expect to have to make that choice. I had never even thought about retiring from the sport. I was in the top two on the team, aiming for my second Olympic Games in Athens.

I don't remember much about that meeting. I reacted in the heat of the moment. Without thinking, I told the coaches that I was done with the sport and walked away. A wave of rage and sadness engulfed me after that. How could they ask me to make this choice? I had always been certain that I could pursue both school and sport.

In the past, teachers were the ones to question my abilities to do so, but my coaches never did, and it really upset me. Why couldn't they allow me to do both? I firmly believe they had no right to do so, but I also felt powerless. They were the ones deciding the team selection.

In retrospect, I should have noticed the signs leading to that request. The coaching staff was less and less accommodating about my study requests. They kept adding additional training hours to our already busy schedule and had no patience for our other endeavors. They barely agreed to a day off for me to attend the exam for school.

The pressure and constant conflict with my coaches combined with eight hours of daily training and late-night studying lead to burnout. During that time, I was constantly fatigued and struggled to stay motivated.

I decided to focus on school, and I left the sport. I stopped abruptly and focused all of my energy on my studies. This really saved me and helped me rebuild not only my motivation but also my confidence and self-worth. It allowed me to move forward and understand that a life after sport exists. I took advantage of every opportunity I had.

First, I interned for Accorhotels and discovered they offered career opportunities specifically for athletes. This led to an apprenticeship with the company where I worked in sponsorships. It was fascinating because I could stay connected to the sport world but see it from a different angle. I worked on projects like the track and field world championships, the French Open of golf, and the Paris candidacy for the 2012 Olympics.

I finally had more free time and used it every minute of the day to do the things I didn't have time for before. I rediscovered Paris and visited every corner and every museum in the city. I worked as a synchronized swimming coach. I built a network of friends outside of my sport, and I did an exchange program in Thailand and traveled extensively throughout Southeast Asia.

Returning to the sport – a different mindset

Three years after leaving my sport, I graduated from business school and transferred to Australia with my company. I continued to work in marketing and sponsorships with Swimming Australia, Basketball Australia, and the Australian Olympic Committee.

To meet new people and build my social network, I decided to compete in the Australian Synchronized Swimming Championships after a three-year break from the sport. I had no expectations and just wished to have fun.

I traveled to the competition in a camper van, stopping at every town possible on the way to the competition, and returned to work the Monday immediately after. That same morning, I got a call from the National Team coach asking if I wanted to swim for Australia. I won the competition… I laughed at the idea and quickly dismissed it, saying I was retired and had a full-time job.

The CEO of Accorhotels called me into his office and offered, to my amazement, to sponsor my athletic career and help me with the immigration process. My colleagues had heard my conversation with the coach, and the news quickly spread. This was an incredible offer, one that I thought I would never receive, especially in a niche sport like synchronized swimming! How could I refuse the opportunity to return to my sport, keep my job, become Australian, and have the chance to compete in another Olympics?

I originally joined the company in Paris as part of a career transition program for athletes. Being a former athlete always raised my profile in the company. In Australia, it was even more of a boost for me because, in this country, sport is king, and athletes are treated like heroes.

For the company, this was an opportunity to promote their support to an elite athlete and their contribution to the sport community. I became an ambassador for the company by sharing my athletic experiences with colleagues and clients.

I returned to "synchro" with a completely different mindset. My main goal was to enjoy my sport and this new experience. I was determined to approach things differently. I was also much more mature and had more experiences outside of the sport. In addition, I felt secure because I had something to fall back on in the event things didn't work out.

I was also less focused on performance and results and more on the process and the people around me. I particularly enjoyed working with my new coaches, who were from Russia and Ukraine. I learned a lot from them, including their views, approach to training, and their cultural background.

I trained mostly on my own in Sydney and would join my teammates in Brisbane or Melbourne every few weeks for training camps. This forced me to approach my training much differently. I turned to other sports to complement my training and gain knowledge from other coaches and experts. I had to learn to balance my schedule to continue performing my work duties.

I relied heavily on the support of my teammates to teach me changes to the routine and hold my position when I wouldn't be there. These athletes did so with incredible class. I can only imagine how difficult it was to have an outsider suddenly take their spot on the team. Yet they never complained or said anything to me.

Life after Sports – reflect on what you have learned

After my second Olympics in Beijing, I retired again… This time for good, on my own terms, and with a great sense of achievement and peace. I returned to my day job and also flourished in other projects. I continued to stay involved in the sport. I created a club in Sydney and coached young athletes. Several of them went on to compete internationally and at the Olympics. I became a

Pilates instructor. I tried and enjoyed many other sports and spent a lot of time swimming in the ocean.

My first retirement from the sport was devastating. I didn't understand why I had to make that choice; it felt so unfair. It made me angry at my coaches and my sport. But I believe it was a blessing in disguise. It changed the direction of my life and forced me to dive deep to rise again. The period that followed delivered so much personal growth and happiness, perhaps as much as the difficult time I experienced before it.

An athlete's journey is marked by many transitions, discomfort, pains, and disappointment but also personal discovery, fulfillment, and celebrations. It is a vibrant and dynamic path that's extremely rewarding. These ups and downs taught me a lot and helped me prepare for anything. I learned to push myself physically and emotionally.

I learned about others through working in a team and through exposure to many cultures and countries. I have developed a fierce belief that I can accomplish anything if I commit to it and work hard enough. These traits are foundational to the person I am today, and I couldn't have discovered them without my sporting journey.

Aside from the self-discoveries, my sport gave me many opportunities and helped me build a better life. I attended a top school, found my first job, and became an Australian citizen thanks to it.

These life-changing experiences are why, like other athletes, I continue to call myself an athlete or, more appropriately, a former athlete, though I have long retired from competitive athletics. These formative events will be with me forever.

Sport has given me chameleon skills or the ability to handle any situation and make the most of it. It has also taught me the joy and importance of learning. I strive to continually better myself in everything I do. I may not be pursuing physical prowess anymore, but I strive to do things to the best of my ability.

Although I created opportunities for myself, I also understand that I have been lucky in my journey. The soul of an athlete is grounded in optimism and gratefulness for the opportunities and support given to you. This core identity - the athlete mindset - will always be with me as a testimony of what I have accomplished, but also as a reminder that I can do anything.

ABOUT MYRIAM

Myriam Glez is a renowned four-time Olympian with an impressive career in Synchronized Swimming. She has competed twice as an athlete and twice as a coach for four countries, including Team France in 2000, Team Australia in 2008, Team GB in 2012, and Team USA in 2016.

After retiring from competitive sports, Myriam worked in sponsorships and marketing for AccorHotels for a decade, gaining valuable experience working in multiple countries. In 2010, she returned to the sports world as a consultant for British Swimming.

In 2013, Myriam took on the role of High-Performance Director and eventually CEO of USA Synchronized Swimming. During her tenure, she led a comprehensive restructuring of the organization, focusing on long-term performance, talent identification, athlete development, and coaches' education.

With a passion for the well-being of athletes and coaches, Myriam founded Athletes Soul, a non-profit organization that supports retiring athletes and raises awareness about the challenges of athletic retirement. Her dedication to creating a positive impact on the lives of athletes and coaches is a testament to her unwavering commitment to the sport and the people involved.

You can connect with Myriam at myriam@athletessoul.org.

CHAPTER 3

THE JOURNEY TO EM-POWERMENT

BY EMILY ESPOSITO

Growing up, I was the little girl that wrote on every single paper that I wanted to be a professional basketball player in the WNBA. Basketball consumed my life. It was my passion. My identity. I had been playing for as long as I could remember, and I was decent at it. I was Emily, the basketball player. Emily, the athlete.

I used to be like many young athletes hoping to play D1 sports; I got up early before school to shoot, do extra training, and start the recruiting process at thirteen.

I spent my four years of high school constantly assessing schools, coaches, and teams, wondering where my next home would be. As some of my high school teachers will tell you, I didn't take the process lightly, but it was exciting. I had this dream of what my college basketball experience would look like, and I was getting so close. And then I did it.

I got to play Division 1 basketball, the one thing I had dreamed of my whole life. However, this lifelong dream of mine panned out much differently than I had imagined. In my five-year college career, I only played one full season on the court. I played for three different head coaches, red-shirted twice, transferred once, and took five years to complete my degree. The further I got into college, I loathed basketball, myself, and my entire experience. Basketball was the one thing I thought I had going for me, and it was anything but perfect.

I started at Villanova in 2017 and was there for two years. By the second year, I began to settle in, and so did dysfunction. I struggled mentally and academically so much that basketball began to feel like a burden, not a blessing.

I felt like I had taken all the lessons and punches that the transition to college could give, and it was starting to negatively affect me and my character.

I remember sitting down with my academic advisor then and telling her that my biggest fear was that I would become a worse person there. I was sleeping all the time, not going to class consistently, and only leaving my dorm room to go to practice or the dining hall.

It was the first time that I felt like I was going through the motions of my day-to-day life to get by. Looking back, I was depressed, but my coaches never asked, and I didn't share.

When I went to class, I had difficulty keeping focused. My mom would tell me that I just needed to apply myself more. I will say this was partly true. I needed to be proactive and find strategies to help myself learn. I remember calling my mom and asking her, "Why am I stupid? Why don't I get these things?"

But my mom, being the woman she is, never bought into that narrative. (Today, I am very grateful for that).

Finally, one day, I took an Uber to a psychiatrist's house on referral from my academic advisor. She ran a series of tests on memorization and comprehension. I felt inadequate. When I got the results about a week later, the report showed learning disabilities, ADHD, and short-term memory issues, and that was just on the first page. I never read the rest because, with every word, I felt my self-esteem fade. I could get extra time on tests, recorded lectures, and shared notes, but I didn't tell anyone.

Though it explains why I struggled to learn the plays as quickly as my teammates, I was too embarrassed to talk about it. I dealt with this silently for the first two years of college. When I transferred to Boston University, that quickly changed.

I think my athletic identity and self-worth changed when I got to BU, but it got better before it got worse. At that moment, it was better because, for the first time, I had made a decision for myself as Emily rather than me as an athlete. However, after that decision, I felt like I lost a lot of support (whether from others or internally) because I had picked a lower-level program to transfer to and was not doing as well in my basketball career.

In the following months, I found it hard not to question myself and my decision to leave Villanova. I felt like all my struggles were because I made the "wrong" decision. I think I subconsciously yearned for the classic college athlete success story filled with championships and accolades. But now, I remind myself that every possible path a person can pick in life is filled with adversity and struggle, and your journey is not always what you think it will be. And going back and changing the decision does not mean that everything will inevitably be better.

The second time I ever went to therapy, my therapist asked me what my hobbies and interests were. I remember taking a long pause. I couldn't think.

I responded, "I'm not sure. I'm not very good at anything besides basketball." And that's how I truly felt.

He responded, "I didn't ask you what you were good at. To have hobbies, you are not required to be good at them. And how do you expect to get good at anything if you never start?"

I didn't know who I was or what I wanted in life without the basketball and the validating trophies that could come with it.

I had these very rigid, conscious expectations of what my college career would look like. And honestly, I've felt that way about most aspects of my life. I didn't fight back when things didn't happen the way I wanted. I allowed myself to be pushed around by the inevitable hardships of life, societal norms, and what everybody else expected of me rather than accepting the idea that I had a role in my own life. I began to play the victim and ask, "why me?" far too often.

In hindsight, I'd like to think that what I should have done was take life as it came. Put on my boxing gloves and fight back. Make my life my own story. I was so caught up in the expectations of what should happen in my life and basketball career that I was losing my agency. When something did not go as planned, I was quick to say my career and story were failures. But how could I even say that when neither my career nor my story had come to an end?

The expectations I placed on myself not only held me down and gave me limits, but they also were generous enough to give me depression. You get to write your story as you go and make it what you want. You are holding the pen and paper to your own life—never forget how powerful that is! You get to pick up the pen when you want, write what you want, and if you're going to start a new page, you have the power to flip to the next one and start writing.

With that being said, keep in mind that what you write every day and how you carry yourself come from the standards you set for yourself. Your standards are what you are okay with and will allow in your life, whether you realize it or not. Your expectations are what you hope for and often represent your ideal outcomes, whatever that may look like.

I've learned that oftentimes we think the value of our stories is found in the trophies, accolades, and accomplishments and that if we don't have enough of them, our stories aren't worth sharing. That could not be further from the truth. There is room for every story; we have to be bold and brave enough to share it. My college basketball career did not come with many championships or accolades, but it is still my story whether I like it or not, and I've come to understand that I must embrace my story to empower myself. I may not have all the tangible accolades I hoped to have within my basketball experience. Still, it turns out, the intangible wins I gained as a person are more empowering than I could have ever imagined.

Here I was, at the tail end of my career, and I chose to quit with a month and a half left in the season, not because of the physical toll, but because of the mental toll. I am kicking myself for even writing this because, as an athlete, we are always told to be mentally tough. We are supposed to push on, move past, and get over things.

Today, I am learning that I did not quit a sport that I love, but rather walked away from a situation that was no longer serving me (and, in turn, I was no longer serving it). In doing so, I feel the most empowered I have ever felt, not because I wanted to leave my sport or because I decided to give up, but because I decided not to give up on myself. Because for the first time in as long as I can remember, I stripped myself of the "athlete" title, looked at myself in the mirror, and said, "I'm gonna be okay." That has been the best decision I've made in a long time because I simply did what was best for me. (By the way, doing what's best for you looks different for everyone, and that's okay!)

The everyday challenges of surviving college have lasted my entire career. However, as time has passed, I have gotten better at adapting to the demanding situations that arise.

You will often hear that one of the greatest struggles of being a student-athlete at the collegiate level is time management. As a student, you have the mental pressure of schoolwork—not just keeping up with it, but doing well at it. Then as an athlete, you have the physical pressure of practice and games. We are supposed to show up every day, ready to give 100 percent.

We are told that basketball (or whatever your sport is) is supposed to be our safe place—where every other problem leaves when you enter the gym. But playing sports in college comes with more responsibilities and pressures than it did when we were kids.

It becomes a job. I even found my worth becoming more and more tied to basketball. There are more rules and regulations around the game than there used to be. You may see your teammates more as peers than friends, and your coaches may see you as a number before they see you as a person, and that's just the truth.

The reality is that it's hard to balance everything. With all the pressure, time commitments, and mental exhaustion, having a thriving social life becomes a challenge. I have learned that it is all about setting my priorities straight and making sure they align with both my personal goals and my team's goals.

It's not only about what you are willing to do but, just as importantly, what you are willing not to do. It's up to you to balance the fun and success of your college athletic career, and the goal is to have them go hand in hand.

Like mine, your college career will come with a lot of variables that make it what it is. But what is most important is recognizing that your college career is really what you make of it. At the end of your playing days, you want to look back and say that you took advantage of every opportunity given to you. You want to be able to say that you went above and beyond. And yeah, sure, you had hard days, but those are the days that helped you grow the most.

Be that person on your team that sets new self-improvement goals every year, not just basketball goals. Be that person on your team that people can go to when they need someone to listen to or to lean on. College athletics is a great place to grow as a person and leader—always keep that in mind.

Some of my closest supporters embraced my decision, while others didn't. My mental health was deteriorating like never before, yet I experienced many people I trusted and looked up to say things like: "Is your mental health actually that bad?" or "Just keep your head down and power through, Emily. Life is hard."

My close circle got slightly smaller with this choice, but I learned to be okay with that. The empowered version of me could not just sit and "power through," because, to me, powering through meant staying silent. I had finally learned to use my voice to advocate for myself and my mental health, and here I was being told to be quiet, to ignore it. And believe me, I thought about it and even tried doing that for some time. I didn't want to be that person—the one to complain, have problems, and make things difficult. The one who is always a handful.

A week or two after I decided to quit my final season, I confided in a trusted family friend on the phone about these feelings. He then told me something that changed my perspective: "Emily, being a handful is going to be one of your greatest assets. You are bold in what you believe in, and never let that waver."

Today, I am beginning to understand that I have so much more to offer than just putting a ball through a hoop. I am learning to empower myself to look in the mirror and to get comfortable saying, "I am proud of you."

You are so much more than this one thing. And maybe wanting to be more than one thing makes me a handful to some, but for me, my hands are full of ideas, growth, and passion for life again.

We are more than our sport. We are our stories.

Basketball has been a large part of my life, but that is not all that I am.

I needed to view myself as someone with something of greater value and worth sharing with the world. I used to allow my story to bully me until I embraced it. Because of my experiences, good and bad, I have looked at life differently. It has required me to pull back the curtain on parts of my life I didn't like or understand, forcing me to rediscover myself. My story is about EM-POWERMENT. Empowering myself and hoping to empower others.

Picking up the pieces of the young, vibrant kid I used to be and transforming that into the person I am today and the better person I hope to become. My story is about inevitable struggle, change, and loss. But it is also about growth, strength, and living life for every single moment. EM-POWERMENT has helped me find my voice.

It has helped me learn to love the sport from a different perspective and to love myself outside of the sport. It has helped me understand that taking up space is okay. You can (and should) take up space in your sport.

But most importantly, know that you are allowed to take up space outside of your sport. I always wanted to be so much more. I didn't know I could, and I didn't know how. But here I am. Empowered…

ABOUT EMILY

Emily Esposito, a native of Gorham, Maine, grew up in a competitive environment with her two older brothers, Chris and Matt. She participated in multiple sports, including softball, soccer, and basketball, throughout high school before focusing solely on basketball. Emily received a scholarship to Villanova University, where she red-shirted her first year and played her second year before transferring to Boston University.

Due to the transfer rules, Emily had to sit out for another year before playing for Boston University, where she faced a shortened season due to COVID. However, she experienced a coaching change the following year, which made it challenging to see eye to eye and feel valued. Emily made the difficult decision to walk away from that situation, which inspired her to start EM-POWERMENT. The idea came to her about a year and a half ago, and she is now working towards turning it into a non-profit organization to improve the world of college athletics.

Emily credits Coach Bowers, who believed in her more than anyone and encouraged her to write a book, for inspiring her to share her story. She dedicates this chapter to Coach

Bowers, as this is just the beginning of her journey. With EM-POWERMENT, Emily aims to empower others to share their stories and create a positive change in the world of college athletics.

CHAPTER 4

THE EVOLUTION OF AN ATHLETE

ALICIA MCCONNELL

I was a high-energy kid. I grew up in Brooklyn, NY, and always ran around with friends, schoolmates, or neighbors, playing games and trying to invent new ones. We played stickball, stoopball, and kickball, and skateboarding was the new cool sport.

My mom tells me what a handful I was when I was a toddler, between taking my diapers off and disappearing into the woods at my grandparent's house, to running straight into the crashing waves of the ocean with no fear. I threw myself into everything. No qualms, no self-doubt, just a glorious embracing of the world's potential that only a three-year-old can have.

My parents were young professionals who joined a tennis and squash club that was seeking new members. Little did they know how that would bring such opportunity, joy, and focus to their children's lives. There were three of us, and we all loved trying new sports. The first time I played squash was like an explosion in my head and body. The twists and lunges, sprints and jumps, the angles I could hit. The exhilaration of swinging as hard as I could at a ball and hearing the smack it made against the wall. I was hooked.

In some ways, looking back, my career has mirrored that first experience of squash: lunges, sprints, jumps and angles, and plenty of smacks against the wall. This is my story of evolution from a professional athlete to a professional career woman and the roller coaster journey of self-discovery.

Being the best became a necessity because it was a direct reflection of my value and worth; anything less than that was a failure, unleashing my overindulgence and self-destructive tendencies. I was unknowingly enmeshed in trying to fit in rather than focusing my energy on trying to understand myself.

As a young girl, I was good at sports from the start. I often played with the boys in a variety of activities. I was the girl who could run faster, hit the ball harder, and throw farther. I stuck out.

I remember a pickup baseball game where one of the kid's dads, who was pitching, moved closer to toss me an easy pitch. I smacked a line drive right at him. He missed the catch, and the ball slammed him in the face. I was mortified, but inside, I thought it was funny because he had assumed a girl wouldn't be able to hit that well.

I was always compared to the guys, though, rather than being viewed as simply a strong female athlete. In Catholic school, being an outstanding athlete seemed to make me odd and unusual to some rather than talented and unique.

I remember challenging the boys' basketball coach, asking why the girls' team couldn't practice on the school court. He looked at me with shock as he explained that this would take time away from the boys' practice—God forbid! So, we had to practice in the dark, dingy church basement gym instead.

In my gut, I knew it wasn't fair, and over time I eventually wore them down until the girls got to practice on the school court! It might have seemed precocious, but I believed in myself and was fortunate that my parents supported and encouraged this self-belief.

My dad was always ready to fight for his family, but I learned more from my mom, who frequently had to fight to be treated equally in her professional career. She was Director of Nursing at a hospital in Brooklyn and continued to elevate her leadership roles as head of divisions to company vice-president, often being the only woman. She was tough and developed a thick skin to survive and thrive.

I'll never forget when she was let go from a position because she was hiring too many women of color. She fought for what was just. A few years later, that same hospital administrator hired her as a VP in his company.

At thirteen, I participated in my first squash tournament, made it to the final, and never looked back. I won a slew of US and Canadian junior titles and the Junior World Championships in 1980. Winning at such a young age was like a shot of adrenaline, and I couldn't get enough. I was addicted.

Competing and winning against boys and men often made me the target of their animosity, which was difficult to deal with at a young age. I wasn't sure how to fight back, so I tried to act tough and self-assured, became fiercely independent, and tried to rely on no one. That helped me deal with the animosity. That helped me win.

Today this would be called micro-aggression. But hearing comments like "You're too good to be a girl" or "You have strong shoulders like a boy" felt awkward to me back then.

These slights made me doubt myself and question my abilities. Was there something wrong with me? Was there something wrong with being tough and good at sports?

I remember coming home from school one day after many boys had roughed me up during a floor hockey game. I didn't understand why they were so angry and giving me such a hard time. Was it just because I was good? It was confusing because I thought that in sports, you just had to try your best and let the results speak for themselves.

I didn't understand all these preconceived notions about boys being one thing and girls being another. I didn't realize I was challenging the "norms." My mom explained that some people might be jealous of my talent and may act in unkind ways, and her belief in me helped counteract the bullying.

These uncertainties motivated me more in my sport, as I felt like I had more control when I was playing. I got to choose the next shot, fake out my opponent, decide when to jump to intercept the ball, or when to sprint down the court for a layup.

Even though I felt so confident and comfortable in my own skin while playing, I still wanted to fit in and be liked. My desire for acceptance started becoming increasingly apparent the more I realized I was different.

My singular focus on excelling in sports wasn't the norm. Girls were supposed to focus on boys and looking pretty. There were so few female athlete role models. Society seemed to want me to be a nice girl, not to challenge the boys, not to be too assertive, and certainly not to make the guys feel threatened. For someone as fiercely competitive and self-determined as I was, that would always be a challenge.

My first year at the University of Pennsylvania was in 1981. I was on top of the world, going to one of the best schools in the country. I was the number one junior, the number one intercollegiate player, and the number one women's squash player in the U.S. So, even though I needed to earn some cash with a part-time job and fit in all the training and competing around that, things were pretty good.

I also discovered lacrosse, and in my first year playing, I made the varsity squad and, in my senior year, the US national squad. My boyfriend had come to Philadelphia with me. He was a squash player as well and a few years older. The excitement of playing on the squash and lacrosse teams, running from class to class, learning new things, meeting new friends, attending parties, and being independent was thrilling. All in all, I seemed to be living a sweet life.

In truth, though, I was playing the part the outside world wanted me to play. When I realized I liked girls as well as boys, my mind and my emotions went haywire, like being on the spin cycle of a washing machine - tumbling around, disoriented, and feeling wrung out.

It's very different now, but when I was at university, society was very homophobic, and I didn't have any role models living happy and successful "out" lives. That feeling of being on top of the world and feeling sure of myself crumbled in a flash. In one moment, I could be confident and happy, and in the next, self-doubt and anxiety would take over.

My daily life became an internal battle of dealing with being attracted to women but outwardly remaining the focused athlete everyone expected me to be. I didn't know how to express any of this, how to deal with my feelings, or even where to start understanding myself. I did what so many smart, competent women did before me. I internalized it and distracted myself with food, alcohol, and sex.

A close friend I grew up with kept calling me to catch up. We finally found a time to meet up, and after a lot of probing from her, I finally admitted that I liked girls. It was a relief to say the words out loud and an even greater relief when she was fully supportive. That gave me the strength to tell my sister, who was also so supportive! Suddenly, I learned it was safe to communicate my feelings and what I was going through to friends and family.

Playing lacrosse also brought me a lot of enjoyment during this difficult time. On the lacrosse field, I didn't feel as much pressure as I did on a squash court, and I was reveling in how much more fun it was to be playing on a team and competing together. To work with others on a joint goal, to support each other in executing plays, and to watch it all come together on the field in a team "win" was exhilarating.

Leading up to and after graduation, I spent a lot of time

contemplating getting a "real job" and feeling pressure to start a "real" career, but I took the plunge and decided to commit to playing squash professionally. That meant putting myself out there to travel, play, and compete against the best in the world - not just the best in the US. I felt that the focus I would need to be a full-time athlete would somehow help still my mind and give me purpose.

So, a few weeks after making my decision, I packed a bag and boarded a plane with just a few dollars in my pocket. I headed for New Zealand and Australia for six months because they were the epicenter of international squash at the time. Other than getting there, I had no real plans. It might seem crazy today, but it was the one thing I knew with certainty that I could do, so I had to try it. I figured that I'd work out the details when I got there.

It was a thrilling adventure to play at this new level, live a new life, experience a new culture, and find people to train with and tournaments to compete in! I sofa-surfed in the homes of strangers who became friends, discovered a new intensity of training and competing, and found a new community filled with wonderful camaraderie.

Ultimately, though, I was there to compete and deliver results. So, I set myself a goal from the very start. I wanted to reach the top sixteen in the world within my first year on the tour.

Since no other American had ever competed on the international tour, I had no benchmark, no idea what to expect, and no idea whether that was even a realistic goal.

In truth, it wasn't a realistic goal, but I didn't know that at the time. I just figured that if I did something no other American had done, I could finally see myself as a success, and I could finally respect myself.

I threw myself into it. I committed to my path, and ultimately… I succeeded.

I did it! I was the first ever U.S. woman to achieve such a ranking on the international squash tour. It was hugely significant because it gave me automatic entry into almost every tournament. That meant prize money (meager, though it was) and being hosted at tournaments rather than relying on the kindness of strangers and their sofas.

It was an amazing moment when the world rankings came out, seeing that I had reached my goal of becoming number sixteen in the world. I felt like the earth should have moved. It was a monumental achievement in my mind, coming from nowhere with little or no support and certainly no entourage to help me get there. I thought this accomplishment was going to change my life. I waited for that tidal wave of elation that would carry me into my future "happily ever after." Spoiler alert: it didn't come.

I don't know why I expected this. It was pretty naïve and a bit crazy—and that's precisely what I realized about 3.6 seconds after the rankings came out. The earth didn't move.

The belief that "I am on my way, I have done enough, I am enough, I am successful" didn't happen. I was in shock. It was a moment of absolute clarity and terror at the same time. Though I continued to play, and my ranking climbed further, the fire was already gone from me, and the realization slowly dawned on me that no matter what ranking I achieved, it wouldn't make me any happier myself. It wouldn't fix me.

Though I still craved fulfillment and a sense of self-worth, I now knew that I would not find that on a squash court, and I recognized that I would not be able to support myself financially by being a professional athlete.

So, after playing full-time for over six years after university, having been number one in the U.S. for seven years, and getting to number fourteen in the world, I retired with no income, a list of nagging injuries that would make a physical therapist blush, and the immediate need to find a job.

Figuring out how to move on is hard. Figuring out what your path should be is hard. Change is hard. I felt so lost leaving my sport because it was all I knew, and it had become how other people and I defined myself.

I did not know how to develop a professional career at the ripe old age of twenty-nine. So naturally, I panicked and took the first job I applied for.

The job I took was at the biggest sporting goods store in NYC. When I was a kid, I loved this store. I used to press my nose against the window and gaze at all the cool gear I longed to own.

I dreamed of getting locked in after hours, letting my buddies in a back door, running amok with all the equipment, and having our own private little Olympics. So, when I saw an advertisement in the paper for a manager, I figured, "what the heck."

They offered me a less than inspiring position as a "rackets specialist." That meant I got to "advise" customers on the best rackets for them.

As an athlete, I was surprised at how exhausting being on my feet all day and dealing with nagging customers was. But at least I enjoyed helping people find exactly what suited them. However, most of the time, the job was draining, the pay was awful, and I felt like I was in a slow-motion nightmare, where I was endlessly searching for equipment that I couldn't find buried in the back of a gloomy storehouse.

One day a customer came into the store, did a double take at me, and asked, "Why are you working here?" He could not miss my gray polyester vest and plain white name tag that not-so-proudly proclaimed "Alicia."

He knew me as a world-class squash player, but now he looked at me with such pity and thinly veiled embarrassment that it broke me. I didn't know what to say.

My inner voice whispered, *Look at you now, look at what you've become*! It hit me hard. After work that day, like every other day, I used my cut-out coupons for a fast-food meal and got on a sardine-packed subway to my tiny, rented room in Brooklyn.

That inner voice that always drove me to train more and work harder now shattered me. It was getting the best of me, telling me, *You are nothing, you are no one, you should have done better, achieved more, and made everyone proud. Instead, you're just a pathetic failure.*

It was so hard to fight that voice because I believed it. I believed I had squandered my talent, had not made my country proud, hadn't valued the opportunities enough. And just as my fellow Penn alum had said, "Why was I even here?"

Even writing this now takes me back to those dismal times

and those visceral feelings of frustration and pain, and even now, I want to scream out, "It is hard; life isn't easy!"

Looking back, that moment was a turning point in my life. I'd love to say I immediately quit my crappy job and made some brilliant and inspired career choices that set me on a path to developing a new product or starting my own business. It didn't quite happen that way, though. Instead, it was a process. It was little steps. It was a humbling experience.

Over the years, I tried a lot of different ways to find my path, purpose, and meaning. I tried to create new meditation and yoga routines and prioritize time with friends and family.

I tried to focus on living in the present, not overanalyzing the past or obsessively worrying about the future. I tried different types of massage therapy and acupuncture and devoured a small library's worth of self-help books. It all helped, but what got me through was finally reaching out to others and asking for help.

I sought out a variety of individual and group counseling sessions, which helped me to understand my tumult of emotions inside. I learned those feelings didn't have to define me, that they are simply part of me and don't need to dictate my reactions.

It was hard to learn to value myself and my accomplishments, practice new behaviors, and let go of my singular identity as an athlete. I had to learn to listen, ask for advice, use my contacts, and open myself up to others.

The drive I had as an athlete led me to learn new skills and tools for leading a more balanced life. I had to practice figuring out what I was feeling and then try to communicate that in more precise ways to friends and family.

It is an amazing new awareness and incredible feeling when I can tell my sister how important she is to me, tell my brother how proud I am of him, and say the words "I love you" to my hardworking mom and dad.

Sharing myself with others taught me I didn't have to internalize everything. It was in being vulnerable that I found strength. It was in admitting my lack of knowledge that I found more clarity. Admitting to weakness and your challenging behavior draws your loved ones closer.

It was a revelation that just being myself with others creates a strong connection of acceptance, trust, and a sense of peace. I would call my mom when I struggled with confidence and motivation, and those conversations helped keep me balanced. I could talk to my sister about anything, and being able to share my insecurities and concerns with her was a game changer. Those calls helped me learn how to turn down the volume of the self-destructive, critical voice inside and instead focus on cultivating a calmer, more patient me.

The same intensity and drive that had helped me succeed in sports had become a protective armor around me. People genuinely want to help and be supportive, and helping others was something that I discovered I enjoyed.

When I taught tennis in NYC to inner-city kids, their smiles after hitting a ball well or learning a new skill were infectious. I loved that feeling of contributing and giving back. I realized that all the awards and winning didn't matter if I couldn't share the experiences with those most important to me. That was where genuine joy lived.

I understood that I needed to become the personal coach I always wanted to be! The coach who has the perfect balance of toughness and patience, clarity and motivation, who knows when to give a hug or confront someone about their stubbornness.

Just as it is essential to have people around you who will be supportive and love you when you don't love yourself, it is also essential to have people, resources, and activities around you that will challenge and inspire you to be better.

I was still the confused "rackets specialist," trying to figure out my life, but then I caught a break. Or rather, I jumped at an opportunity that cropped up and hung on with both hands.

A friend asked me to sub for him to give him some coaching sessions at NYU. Coincidentally, the head of athletics there knew my squash history, and after seeing my work with some students, she offered me a coaching gig.

It was the start of a new journey, one that I didn't realize I had been resisting. I assumed coaching squash wasn't a serious profession. I was so surprised when I discovered I enjoyed teaching others to play the sport I loved. I finally found myself in a space where I was open to change, which transformed everything. After all, coaching set me on my true path without realizing it.

I loved coaching, I enjoyed connecting with so many people and trying to help them learn a new sport, improve their game, or pursue a national rank. Each individual was like a puzzle to me, figuring out what made them tick and what exercises, drills, and games would help them improve and enjoy their game.

I worked hard coaching in a few locations and was overjoyed to be hired as head professional at the Heights Casino in Brooklyn. I was back in the club that started it all for me, and I was able to help them grow their nationally recognized junior program.

My organizational, planning, and social engagement skills came to life in this role. It was a hard job, with extended hours and parents with high expectations, but I felt a strong sense of purpose. I loved being back on the court and giving back too, and I treasured falling in love with squash all over again.

On a rare vacation from the court, I visited a friend in Colorado who had just started working for the U.S. Olympic and Paralympic Committee (USOPC). I loved it there, and when a position arose at the USOPC, I jumped at the opportunity.

I was hired as the manager of Athlete Development, developing and expanding youth programs for underserved populations across the US. It was quite a change working in an office-based environment. It was an area I was deeply passionate about, but being in an office differs significantly from being in the field.

Quickly, though, I discovered that the skills I had learned from the court transferred well, including analysis, goal-setting, and working out a plan to achieve those goals.

My focus, discipline, patience, and organizational skills were all put to good use, and best of all, I was working to help others achieve their goals too. It turns out that all those skills that I had honed on squash courts and playing fields were all abilities that transferred well to the business world.

Things came full circle when I became the director of athletic facilities and services. This role allowed me to create, develop, and implement programs and partnerships to support athletes in achieving their dreams of high performance. I also got to assist athletes as they made their transition to life after sports.

We had a mentor program, resumé-building and financial management classes, one-on-one career counseling sessions, and networking events. We also hosted the first Post-Olympic and Paralympic Summit for athletes who were considering retiring.

My experience helped enormously in understanding these athletes' challenges, and I reveled in the opportunity to help them and others. I embraced finding my way and using my voice to speak up and fight for what I believed in, just as I had on the squash court and playing field.

With a growing sense of confidence, I spread my wings and became embedded in the Colorado Springs community. I sought out and was invited to many leadership programs at the globally renowned Center for Creative Leadership. I was continually educating myself to be of service as a board member for numerous organizations.

I remain proud of the myriad of boards and committees that I served on and the work we did. I am humbled by the many community awards I received for my service, as I wasn't seeking the accolades I had been in squash.

I finally fully embraced my own sexual identity and worked hard to bring more visibility to LGBTQ+ issues in the conservative-leaning community of Colorado Springs.

Thinking about what I have accomplished in life after sports is empowering and brings me a deep sense of joy and fulfillment. Through the hard times, lack of belief in myself, and unhealthy behaviors, I came through it one step at a time. It was through reaching out to family and friends and leaning on the support of therapists, counselors, and the love that people offered and continue to have for me. I like the Alicia I have become.

Yes, I am still fiercely competitive and can get intense and serious about many things, but I know I am also so much more than simply Alicia, the athlete.

Being the only woman in a work meeting, boardroom, golf course, or men's squash tournament can make me feel pressured. But now I welcome the opportunity to be the person in the room who calls out the bias, who can see what is missing, and speak up. I have learned to channel my energy in a healthier and more constructive way.

I have been called "emotional" or "aggressive" for this when I know it is a wonderful talent to be passionate and assertive.

Living in Dublin, Ireland, now with my loving and supportive wife, I am still deeply committed to being a part of my community and passionate about giving back.

What helps me every day is practicing gratitude, understanding that I don't have all the answers, and knowing that friends and family want to be a part of my journey.

Accepting how I respond to life's situations is my choice. To build recovery time into my days and to have other interests, like sculpture, cooking, word games, gardening, and visiting magical places. To make time to have fun and laugh, as I can take myself way too seriously. To have regular calls with friends and family.

Giving back to my community by volunteering on boards and committees and sharing my insights, talents, and ideas.

I had become so used to doing things one way, which was with an unending intensity, and it was tough to learn that everyday life is not that. Daily life can be calmer and more balanced.

Part of my story was learning to reclaim my identity unapologetically. I was often told to be more ladylike, polite, and nice. I can be all those things, but why should I fit into someone else's story? This is my story, and I have learned to love and embrace it.

I am so grateful to many who helped guide me along the way, especially Fred and Carol Weymuller, when I didn't even realize I needed it. Finally, I understand that wonderful African proverb, "If you want to go fast, go alone. If you want to go far, go together."

ABOUT ALICIA

Alicia McConnell is a former elite athlete and coach who has worked in leadership roles across all levels of sports and community service. She served as the Director of Training Sites and Community Partnerships for the United States Olympic and Paralympic Committee (USOPC), where she worked from 1998 to 2019.

Alicia currently resides in Dublin, Ireland, and works as a consultant and advisor on selective projects in sport, particularly in diversity, equity, and inclusion.

At the USOPC, she created opportunities for sport development and access to resources, services, and facilities for athletes and National Governing Bodies of Sport (NGBs) by collaborating with community organizations throughout the United States.

She also broadened the scope of athlete services, particularly for athletes considering retiring from sport, initiated the USOCP and NGB Young Professionals Network, launched the USOCP LGBTQ+ Employee Resource Group, authored the USOPC Youth Sport Development Strategy, and published two athlete research reports.

Alicia is also involved in several community organizations, serving as a Trustee for the Professional Squash Association

Foundation, community lead for Sporting Pride Ireland, and literacy volunteer for DePaul Charities. She has also held leadership positions on several boards, such as Chair of Visit Colorado Springs, Treasurer of the National Council for Youth Sports, and USA Swimming's Diversity Committee, to name a few.

Alicia's achievements as an athlete include winning all three titles of Junior, Intercollegiate, and Women's National Squash Champion at eighteen. She won the World Junior Championships in 1980 and went on to win the US Nationals for seven years from 1981-1988.

She has competed in six world championships and one Pan American Games, winning silver and bronze medals. Alicia held the National Women's Squash Doubles title from 1996 through 2006.

In recognition of her leadership and service, Alicia has received several awards, including the Women's Leadership Program Award from the J.P Morgan Tournament of Champions in 2021, the "ATHENA" International Award from the Colorado Springs Business Alliance in 2017, and the President's Cup from US Squash and the Diversity and Inclusion Award from the Colorado Springs Independent in 2015.

She was named "Woman of Influence" by the Colorado Springs Business Journal in 2013 and a "Woman of Distinction" in 2007 by the Girls Scouts. She was also a Mentor for the U.S. Department of State and ESPNW's Global Women's Sports Network Program.

Alicia is a member of three Halls of Fame, including the inaugural class of the University of Pennsylvania Hall of Fame in 1996, the inaugural class of U.S. Squash's Hall of Fame in 2000, and the Intercollegiate Squash Hall of Fame in 2001.

Connect with me on LinkedIn @ Alicia McConnell.

CHAPTER 5

A TRANSITION FROM WITHIN

*"Never breathe life into mediocrity,
always give your best."*

BY JACKIE SMITH

On a chilly day in Queens, New York, my mother called me in and scolded me, saying, "Girl, don't you have sense to come in from the freezing cold? It's 30 degrees out there."

I had been playing basketball for over an hour. I was standing there, shivering, and my fingers were close to crinkling and bent from frostbite. At that moment, at eight years old, I declared to her that I would be a collegiate athlete and that neither she nor my father would have to worry about paying my tuition. I was going to become a professional basketball player. I practiced hard. I was coachable and disciplined, and my declaration became my reality.

Being the youngest of five siblings gave me plenty of opportunities to skip chores and run out the front door with my ball in hand, down the steps, take one hop over the fence, and dash across the street to the park. I can't count the number of times I was nearly hit by a car.

I was always so excited to play and practice from sunup to sundown in just about any weather condition. I have many fond memories, but now I am a retired athlete who must make new memories. What I didn't realize on that freezing day when I prophesied my future was that I didn't include my transition from basketball as part of the picture. Transition coaching in the '90s didn't exist; organizations like Athletes Soul didn't exist. I was all alone to figure out my transition plan.

I thought I would be the athlete who would play until my legs couldn't move anymore, and then a career would be dropped in my lap. I was a talented student; everyone was always telling me I must have good grades and do well in school, but there wasn't anyone in my ear telling me about careers and sports jobs other than coaching basketball.

I was only concerned about getting into college, getting a scholarship, and becoming a professional basketball player in another country. This was the pre-WNBA era. That was it! I didn't think of the uncertainty of my life in the future. I did not know I would be so unprepared when I left the game. I became a retired athlete with no plan for the next chapter in my life.

Reality check

I searched for a job repeatedly, not making it past the interviewing process. I became increasingly frustrated, losing confidence and hating the fact that there was no place for me to belong. Why didn't people appreciate that I had put so much time into learning my skill and that my skills were transferable if given an opportunity to prove it?

After playing college basketball, my teammates pursued their careers and slowly left the sport. As for me, I received an offer to play professionally in Paris, France, so basketball was very much alive for me until I came home. I felt punished for pursuing professional basketball and left without a career path.

My teammates didn't talk about adjusting to life after basketball. They naturally just conformed to getting a job right after college; meanwhile, I struggled because I chose a different path. It wasn't that easy for me.

The routine of having no routine made me so melancholic. I was used to getting up, working out, and concentrating on getting one percent better every day, but after my retirement, my days were filled with emptiness and no purpose. I would still play basketball and enjoy it immensely, but there was no endgame, no goal other than to win the game in front of me.

One day, I recall driving and feeling sad, disappointed in myself, and feeling lost. So, I called my mom and asked her, "Is this it for me? Am I done with my purpose?"

She was so worried. She could tell I wasn't in a good place, and all she wanted was for me to come home. I cried like a baby on the phone, and yes, I had all kinds of crazy thoughts, even suicidal thoughts, but my love for my family took me home, where I wept in her arms once again.

My first job was at the Brooklyn Sports Foundation. We were developing a sports arena for amateur sports in Brooklyn, NY, which was much needed. The biggest arena for amateur sports was St. John's University, and track and field events were held in armories.

I felt like I was doing something important. I loved that job, the politics, and all the wonderful people I met on the journey.

But it didn't last. Politics killed the project, and what was a possibility was no more. Personal conflicts stood in the way of the needs of athletes to reach their fullest potential in a first-class facility. We received funding from the State; however, the New York City government could never get on the same page. Self-interest, personal conflict, and egos all contributed to the demise of a state-of-the-art, multi-purpose facility for amateur sports.

It was a sad day when the Brooklyn Sports Foundation closed its doors. A sad day for the Mayor of New York, New York City elected officials, and Brooklyn politicians who missed the opportunity to do something great for amateur sports in the city and borough. And most of all, a sad day for athletes.

During all the chaos and uncertainty in my future, my family and I were struck with a deadly blow to our family structure. My father was diagnosed with stage four colon cancer. He passed away two years later. I was devastated, heavy-hearted, and felt like everything was falling apart.

My parents were always my biggest supporters. They traveled everywhere to see me play. I wanted my father to see me become a coach. But, instead, I had to envision him watching me from above in Heaven.

His death made my transition even worse; I became reclusive and stayed close to my mother. She had an on-and-off relationship with a rare disease that nearly took her life several times since my birth. I couldn't fathom her leaving me. With so much going on, I was an emotional wreck.

I was blessed to start a head basketball coaching position at York College in Queens, NY. During my coaching career, I was named Coach of the Year, won a CUNYAC Championship, and was inducted into the Hall of Fame for NYC Public Schools Athletic League and St. John's University.

However, I was still adapting to life outside of competitive basketball. My coaching job was part-time, and I needed additional income and a long-term plan for a career. I was still stuck as to what would be my next career. Coaching college basketball was a strong option to continue, but it wasn't in the cards for me. It wasn't because I didn't want to or didn't have success—I enjoyed coaching and was very successful—but because there were significant challenges and changes heading my way that would test my strength and courage.

Soon, another opportunity came along. I was invited to the Harlem Globetrotters tryouts in Orlando, Florida. This was huge, and I was excited. I had two weeks to prepare and worked hard on all my razzle-dazzle tricks. Then, one day, I was riding home from practice on my bike, and I was hit by a car and thrown up in the air.

I distinctly remember thinking, *Don't hit your head, don't hit your head.* Miraculously, I landed on my feet and started dusting off my yellow outfit. My bike was destroyed, and the handlebars were almost completely separated from the bike. I wiped off my clothes and then collapsed.

I was taken to the hospital, given a neck brace, and then sent home after an evaluation. Thank God I had no broken bones. Convinced that I was healthy enough to continue training, I eventually headed to Orlando to try out for the team.

In Orlando, I was treated like a celebrity. I had access to the best of everything; the best food, accommodations, parties, photo ops, press conferences, you name it. I was thrilled when I made the final cut.

It was between another female athlete and me, Jolette Law. We later became friends, but it was a war on the court, and we competed to the very end. Unfortunately, I was disqualified by the Harlem Globetrotter's medical doctors. They were concerned that my body would not be able to sustain a schedule of over 200 games after having a major accident in the prior two weeks.

And just like that, I was transitioning from sports again. I was grateful for the opportunity, and yet sad again because the gut-wrenching feeling of being stuck in an abyss had returned.

Things only got worse.

Triple whammy

My misfortune was compounded by an autoimmune disease that affected my kidneys. I faced three transitions: life without basketball, life without my father, and now a newly diagnosed disease.

This was a battle I knew nothing about. I was depressed. To my knowledge, there was no playbook or strategy to help me get through this. I stayed close to home, and my mother and sisters supported me emotionally the best they could.

After my father's death, I moved back home to support my mother, who was always my biggest fan and my everything. But I didn't realize, at the time, that I would soon need her help as well.

After returning home, I was diagnosed with kidney sarcoidosis, which is a rare inflammatory disease. It causes inflammation, the formation of sarcoid "granulomas" (very tiny nodules or bumps) in the kidney, and kidney stones, to name a few symptoms. I also had so much pain in my joints that I could barely walk. I couldn't believe I was the same elite athlete who had played professional basketball. I was in shock and disbelief that my body was failing me.

It all started when I noticed I was losing weight even though nothing about my normal routine had changed. Next came the profuse sweating, particularly at night. The sweating would get so bad that I changed my shirt numerous times per night.

One evening, I had a temperature, and it was rising quickly. When it approached 102.5°, I knew it was time to seek medical attention. By the time I reached the hospital, my temperature had further increased to 103.5°, and when I was admitted, it was 104°.

The hospital staff went to work trying to break my fever. When they finally did, it was replaced with chills that caused my body to shake so badly it was impossible to even hold a cup. Then the fever and sweating would return. This cycle replayed around the clock while the doctors were searching for a diagnosis.

One morning I woke up and found that my legs were swollen to at least three times their normal size. It terrified me. I wobbled down to the nurse's station and screamed, "Look at me, look at me, what's wrong with me?"

The nurses just stared at my legs in disbelief and paged the doctors on shift. When they arrived, not only were they at a loss as to what was causing my symptoms, but they also shared that

75

my blood platelets were depleted. I now required an immediate blood transfusion.

At this point, my fear peaked because the doctors didn't have a clue as to what was wrong with me. They had guesses and suspicions of lymphoma or tuberculosis, but with every negative test result, it was clear they were grasping at straws. Meanwhile, I was getting sicker and sicker. I knew I had to take my healthcare into my own hands.

When my mother arrived to visit me, I asked her to contact our family doctor, Dr. Charles. Dr. Charles had been my family's physician for decades. He was an excellent doctor, and I trusted him.

As it turned out, Dr. Charles was affiliated with the hospital I was in. He came to see me, looked at my chart, and instantly knew that it most likely was kidney sarcoidosis.

It was confirmed with a few tests. I was treated with high doses of a steroid and was finally able to go home a month later. Sarcoidosis is still an enigma to doctors today, and kidney sarcoidosis is rare. This was a tough period in my life, as I had always been so healthy. But I was so very grateful I was on the road to recovery.

The move

It was my mother's last battle. She was diagnosed with a rare form of terminal cancer, and she wanted to move from New York to my sister's house in Fredericksburg, Virginia. My sister bought a beautiful home for all of us. It was spacious, and we had everything we needed to accommodate us and my handsome flat-coated retriever, Morocco.

Still, I thought my mother had lost her mind, deciding to leave New York, leaving home behind for a strange, new world. I would know no one. No one knew me or my accomplishments. I was truly going to have to start over, redefining myself totally. And I didn't know where to start or whom to ask.

Although moving was the last thing I wanted to do, I couldn't abandon my mother when she needed me most. I went kicking and screaming, but I went. She passed away a little over six weeks later. And there it was, my two favorite people on the planet, my parents, were gone. I was left to mourn while trying desperately to figure out what to do next.

Looking back, I didn't know my life would be so difficult after leaving sports. There was no one I could talk to or look to for guidance. No one showed me how to prepare for my next chapter. I was alone, feeling stuck and left behind.

I didn't know how to share exactly what I was going through. Heck, I didn't even fully understand what I was going through. There were no words I could use at the time to express the anxiety I was feeling about my future. I was angry with myself.

I was angry because I didn't prepare for life after sports. I thought very little about the career I wanted to partake in. And I didn't focus on other areas of my life because basketball made me the happiest. I worked on mastering basketball, but I mastered nothing else, and now I had to start all over again.

I had lost my identity; I thought basketball defined me. I had a tough time finding a career or job. Meanwhile, I lost confidence, and my self-esteem was shot to hell. I was depressed and felt stuck. I wanted something else for myself, but I did not know how to go about getting it.

I finally found joy and purpose when I was hired as the Teen Director of a Boys & Girls Club. As a Teen Director, my primary responsibility was serving as an advocate for teen members and providing after-school tutoring and career/higher education guidance.

A few things I taught teens were social skills, etiquette, career exploration, and money management. We bonded and went on field trips, volunteered at homeless shelters, and went on college tours. My time at the Boys & Girls Club will always be a memorable time in my life because it was there that I learned that helping others wasn't only good for others; it also made me a better person. It felt good, gave me a sense of renewal, belonging, and purpose, and boosted my self-esteem.

Later, I got married to a kind, loving, and supportive person who has been my rock since the day we met. Looking back, I am grateful that I decided to move from New York. If I hadn't, I would never have met my spouse and the talented kids I could help along the way.

A change is coming

In June 2015, I began experiencing gastrointestinal issues. It started with nausea and a general feeling of unwell and progressed to an inability to keep food down within weeks. At that point, I knew it was time to see a doctor, and I'm glad I did.

I was diagnosed with stage one stomach cancer, and I was blessed that it had been caught early. Because of this, no chemo or radiation was required. My doctor, Mark Duncan. M.D., Chief of Surgical Oncology at Johns Hopkins Bayview, gave me two choices: 1) I could have a surgery where the cancer would be cut out along with about half of my stomach to increase the chances of getting it all (it would save my life; however, if the cancer returned, there would be nothing that could be done), or 2) I could do nothing and be dead within three years. I chose the former.

A cancer diagnosis has been my greatest fear since as far back as I can remember. I had seen it claim too many lives. So, when I was first diagnosed, I was devastated and afraid, but deep down, I knew that if I was to survive, I had to accept it and fight. And that's exactly what I did.

I started by examining and challenging my mindset and beliefs, what I believed about myself, and how I spoke to myself. Instead of taking on the role of the victim and complaining, I chose to breathe life into myself.

I learned to forgive myself and others, to let go of things that no longer served me. I learned that some things I thought about myself simply weren't true, like not being good enough, smart enough, or capable. I learned that change takes courage and perseverance. *Becoming* is a journey. You must do the work. Just like you must do the work to lose weight or learn a new skill set.

Later, I was introduced to meditation, which became a daily practice for me. When stress, anxiousness, or worry showed up, I would take time to meditate by simply focusing on my breath and just being in the present moment. Meditation helped restore my inner calm and peace and kept me grounded.

I also read, took long walks in nature, danced, laughed, prayed, and cried during my recovery. But I recovered. I am thrilled to share that I've been cancer free for six and a half years. I am still working on becoming the highest version of myself, but today I am happier because I've learned that happiness is an inside job. It's a choice.

I've also become an entrepreneur, realizing that I simply was not cut out for the typical 9-to-5. It's not in my makeup, my DNA. I now spend my days doing what I love, which is meeting and serving people by helping athletes transition into new careers and make a living in the health and wellness space.

If I had to talk to my younger self coming out of transition or the athletes who are dedicating their lives to sports, here is what I would say:

Never define yourself as just an athlete and by the sport you play. You have so much to offer the world. Your dedication and commitment to sports are just one aspect of your life. Have a big identity. Find other activities that make you feel fulfilled. You are constantly reinventing and redefining what's important in your life, so don't stay in one place doing one thing for too long. Move along. We are here to experience.

Obtain new vocational skill sets that will take you into the future. Be marketable, coachable, and adaptable.

Understand your strengths and weaknesses outside of sports.

Build and cultivate strong relationships with people who can help you with your personal growth, like your coach helped you in sports. There are also mental performance coaches, mentors, business coaches, family, and friends.

Exercise stress management skills to learn how to control stress and anxiety adequately.

Develop a new structure and routine to help you replace your practice routine.

Grow mentally and spiritually and stay grounded. Have faith always.

I read once that tranquility is a process. Try and remember that everything does not have to be figured out immediately.

Reach out to fellow teammates and stay connected with them. You are not alone. Perhaps through sharing, you'll learn how they are dealing with their transition.

Be open to all possibilities and see yourself living the life you desire. Imagine!

Transition is new beginnings, new experiences, and new ways of living. Be courageous, become an explorer, and get comfortable with the unknown because it will lead you to a renewed and revitalized life.

When you become an athlete, the transition from sports is inevitable. Afterward, you must stretch yourself again to become the best version of yourself once more. The pain and difficulty ease when you have a surrendered state of mind and have realized that sports are just one aspect of your life. There is so much more to you, more to accomplish, and many chapters to your life. You can find peace, happiness, and joy in your transition.

Today, I have no regrets because of what I have been through. - all of it - has shaped and molded me. I love who I am, and I love my life. We live in South Carolina now, near my parent's hometown and closer to my siblings and other family members. I am blessed beyond measure.

I have won; I have lost; I have battled sickness, and I have survived loved ones' deaths. I have battled myself, and I am still here. So, don't settle for who you were yesterday. There is no limit to becoming "you!"

I am grateful for the opportunity to share my story. I hope it will help many athletes and people who face the challenge of changing from one life goal to another.

There are many people to thank for this becoming a reality. I would like to thank, in no particular order, Cassandra Warren, Cynthia Smith, Lynn Tucker, Harolyn Smith, Robert Zeig, Richard Williams, Samuel Lipford, Allen Smith, Jarvis Bailey, Tom DeMartino, Ricky Hardin, Rendale Hanas, Ray Butler, The Spinx Company LLC, and Athletes Soul. Your support is invaluable, and I appreciate you in more ways than you can ever imagine.

ABOUT JACKIE

Jacqueline "Jackie" Smith, a Queens, New York native, has been a basketball player since the age of eight. Her unwavering focus and remarkable talent led her to become a celebrated player of international renown, including being the first Pegasus Award winner in New York City, induction into the NYC Public High School Leagues Hall of Fame, and induction into the St. John's University Hall of Fame.

Jackie attended St. John's University, where she earned her bachelor's degree in Criminal Justice. During her time at St. John's, she won two Big East Championships, the Cheryl Miller Women of Distinction Award, and was a two-time MVP ESPN Miller Award recipient, as well as a two-time Big East All-Conference Team member, to name a few of her accolades. As a professional basketball player in Paris, France, she competed in the European Cup and made the All-Conference Team.

Jackie's passion for basketball extended to coaching, and she transformed the women's basketball program at York College in Queens, NY, earning her the Coach of the Year Award. She then continued her coaching career as an Assistant Coach at Hunter College, leading the team to a CUNYAC Conference Championship.

Throughout her career, Jackie has always been committed to the community. She received the Community Service Award from Commissioner of Boxing, Rosa Trentman, and New York State Assemblyman, Clarence Norman, Jr. She is also a recipient of the "Women Dared to Be Different" award from former New York State Congressman, Edolphus Towns, and the Everlast Sports Award for Women's History Month.

Today, Jackie is a personal basketball trainer, mindset coach, and transition coach with Athletes Soul, where she continues to mentor and coach athletes to develop both their player skills and transition into life after sports. Jackie is married and resides in Greenville, South Carolina. She is passionate about helping athletes build a robust and healthy mindset to create a life of abundance in every aspect of their lives.

CHAPTER 6

CAREER-ENDING INJURY

BY KELSEY RUFFING

It was October 30, 2004, when that first "pop" rang out. Every injured athlete remembers the exact date of their injury, and the distinct sound it makes. It's a vivid reel that plays in your head every time you tell the story. This "pop" was the type of sound that made you cringe.

It was also the type of sound you never want to hear on the playing field. I was a 14-year-old forward playing for my travel soccer team, coming into my own as a serious player. I had just started my freshman year of high school and was looking forward to trying out for the high school soccer team in the spring.

I can remember the day, that moment in time, in great detail, and that exact moment when I had torn my anterior cruciate ligament (ACL). The defender and I kicked the ball at the exact same time; a loud pop rang out, and I was on the ground.

I remember feeling scared. I knew that something had to be very wrong. I was crying, holding my right knee and the game had come to a stop. My mother remembers me looking "as white as a ghost." I was able to walk off the field (in my mind, a good sign). I calmed down, bent my knee a few times, and seemingly "just shook it off". I had never experienced an injury in my eight years of playing at that point, and it never crossed my mind that it could happen. Regrettably, I re-entered the game and right away I remember getting tackled. My leg also gave out a time or two during the last few moments before the final whistle blew. I went home and packed some ice on my knee, not knowing what the following day would bring.

As I awoke that next day, I was absolutely horrified to see my knee had swollen to the size of a volleyball; there was no kneecap to be found. I army crawled from my bedroom to my parents' room, unable to walk.

After a doctor's appointment and a few MRI scans, I would learn that my ACL in my right knee was torn and I would need surgery to fix the damaged ligament. This surgery would involve a ligament replacement, weeks of crutches, physical therapy, knee stabilizers, braces, and, worst of all, no spring soccer tryouts.

This was my first serious injury, my first surgery, my first time on crutches, my first time in physical therapy, my first time with anesthesia, and my first time facing any adversity. This was when I started to learn what grit was, and how to be resilient. This was when I began to be serious about motivation and determination. There was not a moment that I doubted myself. I knew I would be back on the field, and perhaps, I was a little naïve to the injury itself, but I knew this would be a bump in the road that I would have to just get over.

Looking back at that first injury and recovery, my positive attitude and mindset fostered a quicker-than-normal healing process and fueled my desire to play harder. My recovery was only four months long.

I had surgery in November and was recovered by March, cleared to play that spring season. It turns out that when the surgeon went in to examine the damage, the ACL had started to mend itself, so he cleaned up the surrounding area and let it heal on its own. I completed twelve weeks of physical therapy and received a very large titanium brace to wear during play.

This was another adversity moment, playing with a brace. The brace slowed me down. As a fast-moving forward I had to figure out how to make this brace work for me and not against me.

I quickly figured out that some defenders were afraid of the brace and afraid of injuring me. Some defenders found out the brace did not feel good on their legs and would shy away. My athlete identity had changed, but I was feeling confident and strong, and then it happened again.

My second ACL tear (left knee this time) came in the winter of 2005. Almost a year exactly to the day of my first. During the first drill of the first day of basketball tryouts, I went up for a layup and the world stopped. Everything slowed down and became quiet. I felt a slight brush against the back of my left knee (the foot of the girl defending me), and I heard that terrible sound of a tear. I heard nothing else.

I could see the faces of a few men on the next court over, looking over in my direction like something terrible had happened. It had. When my slow-motion experience had sped back up to real-time, I was laying on my back, holding my left knee and screaming in pain, "not again, not again."

Concerned faces gathered and my mother was called back to the gymnasium by the coaches, letting her know I had been injured. I remember her face when she walked in, an empathetic sadness. I remember her saying, "maybe it's not the same thing." I think she was hoping that would be the case, but truly knew what we were facing.

We scheduled surgery in late November. I turned 16 that same month and sat for my learners permit before my surgery day. I failed my first attempt. Looking back at this, my head was not in the right mental space for my learners permit exam.

I remember feeling unfocused and uneasy. I was worried about my upcoming surgery, concerned about my recovery, and feeling a little less motivated than previously. This second injury did not bring with it the naivete of the first injury. I knew what to expect and I knew it was not going to be easy by any means.

This surgery resulted in a complete ACL replacement and a few months of physical therapy. I utilized a machine that helped to bend my leg three times a day for three hours at a time. I learned how to walk again, kick again, and had to work a little harder this time to build my confidence and resiliency.

After this recovery, which took about seven months, my father signed me up with a trainer at a sports fitness facility where I could build muscle and work on my conditioning. I gained fifteen pounds of muscle in three months, learned how to meet new nutritional goals for a more powerful performance, and overall, built a great amount of confidence. I knew my strength and was secure in my agility. I knew I was powerful and a threat.

After missing my sophomore soccer season due to the second ACL injury, I was able to play my junior year, feeling the best I had ever felt. That season, I scored the most goals I had ever scored in a season and also led with assists. I never doubted myself, not once. My mental game and physical game were in alignment, and I had the stats to back it up.

I felt proud of my accomplishments, and I was proud about overcoming adversity. Then, at the end of the season, we played in a tournament before playoffs were to begin. I bet you can guess where this is going.

It was May 2007 when I tore my ACL in my right knee again for the second time, resulting in my third ACL tear. The game had just begun, and I was passed the ball, which was not filled completely with air. I stepped on top of the ball and my foot sank. I heard the most bone-chilling sound; to this day I cannot describe it without getting the chills.

As I laid with my face in the dirt, crying, screaming in pain, I heard a girl on my team say, "Oh my god, I think her leg snapped in half." Exactly what you do not want to hear with your face in the dirt screaming in pain.

I was afraid to look at my knee at that point. What I remember even more so was the athletic trainer who came out onto the field to evaluate my knee. She distinctively told me I had not torn my ACL. I looked her in the face and told her I did and she did not know what she was talking about. When you know, you know.

I was sitting on the bench with ice on my knee when I tried to call my mom to let her know. She answered the phone surprised to hear from me and asked what I was doing calling her. She knew I was at a tournament playing. I started to well up and could not get the words out to her. I hung up. She called back, and I mustered enough air to say, "I did it again."

She knew right away what it had meant, and I handed the phone to my coach so she could fill her in. My mom picked up my dad from work and they drove two hours to the fields to pick me up and take me to the ER. That was a very long and silent drive home.

May 12th, my half birthday, I had my third ACL surgery - a complete replacement. This recovery was the most heartbreaking and took the most time. I was cleared to play 9 months later physically, but mentally, I was unsure. Tryouts for the high school soccer team were in March and I had packed my bag with my gear, expecting to attend. When the school bell rang that day, I took my bag, walked to my car in the parking lot, and drove away.

I knew I was not ready, and I knew my heart was not in it enough anymore to possibly face another injury. Looking back on this injury and recovery, I realize now that I had experienced depression and had struggled with my identity as an athlete who was no longer active. Overall, I felt a lack of purpose and like I was just going through the motions every day. I was not particularly excited or thrilled about things I used to enjoy.

My mood seemed apathetic at best. I was at a place in my high school career where I was looking at colleges and trying to figure out a future and had no idea who I was or what I wanted to do. All I had known for so long was my sport, and now it was over.

I attended East Carolina University in the fall of 2008 and declared a major in communications. I always enjoyed writing and was the sports editor for my high school paper. I thought it would be intriguing to be a sideline sports analyst like Pam Oliver or Erin Andrews.

Looking back at my college decision I have to say it was one of my first experiences of truly following my gut. I had only applied to two or three schools and somehow, I "just knew" ECU was a good fit. This decision would open the door for me to experience my first sport psychology class (more on this later).

In the summer of 2009, after my first year of college, I started an internship for the AA affiliate of the New York Yankees. This was an opportunity I found by searching on the internet one day, and again had followed my intuition and applied. I thought this would look great on my CV for future communication gigs. I did all the intern duties you could think of, like pulling the tarp on rainy days (of course it was the stormiest summer that year), selling merchandise, and even dressing up as the mascot at events.

One day at the field, a very important-looking gentleman caught my eye. He was talking with the players, and I had never seen him before. I asked someone who he was, and they told me he was the Sports Psychologist for the Yankees. I was intrigued enough to go up to him and introduce myself (yet another opportunity that my gut pushed me towards).

I asked him about his job as a sports psychologist and told him a bit about my history as an injured athlete. He gave me his email and I made sure to follow up with him to learn more about how he was able to become a sports psychologist. That fall when I returned to school, I changed my major to psychology and minored in sports studies.

Everything he was saying resonated with me in a way that made me believe my purpose was to help athletes who had gone through experiences similar to my own. I knew sports psychology was the career I was going to pursue. The passion in me was once again ignited.

After graduating with my bachelor's degree in Psychology, I attended Adler University in Chicago, Illinois, where I received a Master's in Counseling and Sport and Health Psychology. I chose this program because, at the time, there were limited master's programs specializing in Sport Psychology. I was not sure I wanted to enter a doctoral program right away, and this two-year program felt like a commitment I could make.

This particular program also trained students to become licensed as a therapist in the state of Illinois. This was important to me for two reasons: 1) I could fall back on counseling if/when necessary, and 2) I was able to help athletes from a clinical perspective and a mental skills perspective (which I believed made me more marketable in the field). My wants, dreams, and professional desires aligned with what the program had to offer, and Chicago felt like the right place to be. Again, I listened to my intuition.

There is a theme that plays throughout my professional endeavors; I followed my intuition. I trusted my gut. When I made decisions, I made them in confidence and kept moving. It is often the case when mentoring young professionals that they are afraid to make choices. They tell me they want to "make the right decision," often leading to hesitating in making any decision at all.

When I made the decision to study communications at the onset of my bachelor's degree, it was the best choice at that time, but ultimately, it brought me to sport psychology. The key is to just choose, make a decision, and then make another and another - but build upon your intuition along the way. Get to know yourself and what fuels you. Your decisions should help you get to know yourself so you can ultimately get to where you want to go. Looking back, I realize I followed what sparked my interest and was driven by a passion that guided my decisions.

After graduating with my master's degree, I went into my professional career feeling motivated and excited, but very unsure about how to establish myself in the sports psychology field, especially with limited experience. The program did not have a class on business development, and it felt like we were released into the wild and left to figure it out the hard way.

I joined a private practice and worked primarily in mental health, with a few athlete clients sprinkled in my caseload. After two years in the working world, I felt the desire to go back to school and pursue my Psy.D. in psychology. I missed academia and the opportunities that come with it, like meeting like-minded people with similar interests, conferences, internships, and such. I also thought pursuing a doctoral degree would help me be taken more seriously in the field. So, in the fall of 2016, I began my doctoral program at Adler University.

During this five to seven-year program, I would experience adversity again, but not in the athletic realm; this adversity was related to my health. And I found myself tapping into the same characteristics that allowed me to push through my previous injuries and surgeries.

I had back surgery during my first year in the program, and simultaneously was diagnosed with an autoimmune disease (which explained the symptoms I had been experiencing for an extended period of time). I could relate what I was experiencing mentally and emotionally with my chronic illness to how I had felt mentally and emotionally with my ACL injuries.

There was a grieving process for both and a question of personal identity: "Who am I now that I have this?" "What does this mean for me?" What is even more interesting is that while I was experiencing chronic pain and chronic illness, I was in a clinical psychology program specializing in primary care and behavioral medicine, working with individuals who were experiencing chronic pain and chronic illness. The answers to these questions were the same as they were years prior. Sometimes life throws you for a loop so you can expand and grow.

I do not believe in coincidences. Everything I have experienced in life I try to use to help empathize and relate to my clients in order to help them overcome their own difficult situations. It was during this time in my graduate program that I started to realize the meaning of my injuries and retirement from sport.

The meaning-making was the key in the process of overcoming. When we make meaning of our difficult circumstances, we find ourselves on the other end of grief.

My therapeutic outlook and my philosophy on overcoming adversity have been built on this very concept. When we take our most difficult moments and make them the stepping stones of our successes, we thrive. It truly is not about what happens to us, but how we make meaning of our experiences and use them to our advantage in order to live more fulfilling lives.

When I think about the soul of an athlete, I think about this; how we use the very characteristics that make us athletes (grit, determination, tenacity, courage) even when the game is done, even when we have hung up the cleats. These characteristics stick with us and can propel us into the next chapter of our lives.

ABOUT KELSEY

Kelsey Ruffing, MA, MS, LCPC, is an accomplished Licensed Clinical Professional Counselor (LCPC) with extensive expertise in chronic pain, illness, and sports injury. As the owner and CEO of Kelsey Ruffing Counseling, Kelsey provides cutting-edge therapy centered around the mind-body connection.

Kelsey's academic background includes a Master of Arts in Counseling with a specialization in Sport and Health Psychology from Adler University (2014), a Master of Science in Clinical Psychopharmacology from The Chicago School of Professional Psychology (2019), and a Master of Arts in Clinical Psychology from Adler University (2018).

Kelsey's passion for sports began at an early age, and she excelled in multiple sports throughout her youth. She focused heavily on soccer and had to retire from sport her senior year of high school after experiencing three ACL tears in four years. Her personal experience with sports injury inspired her to pursue a career in counseling, where she now specializes in helping athletes who have undergone similar experiences.

Kelsey is committed to providing the highest level of care to her clients, and she uses a holistic approach to address their unique needs. With her extensive education and practical experience, Kelsey is a leading authority in her field and is highly respected by her peers and patients alike.

CHAPTER 7

CONQUERING THE RACQUET WORLD

BY BELLINA BARROW AND SHERDON PIERRE

Sports came full circle for me. I was raised in a nuclear family in Arima, Trinidad and Tobago, West Indies. I was born in the country's capital city of Port-of-Spain but grew up in Arima.

My early schooling was at Arima New Government School. The Royal Chartered Borough of Arima is home to many sporting clubs and accomplished sports personalities (like other parts of Trinidad and Tobago). In recent years, it boasts of being host to the "We Run Arima 5k," which is the largest distance running event in Arima. However, my claim to fame is not running, but another sport entirely!

The gift that keeps giving

Some of my early Sunday mornings were spent riding down the Priority Bus Route (PBR) with my father, Ronald Barrow, of blessed memory. I also accompanied him and a couple of his closest friends to the Queen's Park Oval, Port-of-Spain, to spectate and support the West Indies Cricket Team during their matches (more so test matches than one-day matches).

At that time, the shorter versions of the game—the Caribbean Premier League and all the different permutations of the shortened game—were not even a thing as they are now. It was through my introduction and immersion in sports at such a young age that I developed a love and appreciation for sports and for representing my country and region well.

My father introduced me to the sport of table tennis when he purchased a table tennis board for the family as a Christmas gift. While I was involved in multiple sports and extra-curricular activities as a child, including lawn tennis, cricket, basketball, swimming, and chess, I zeroed in on table tennis in the early 1990s.

Before formally taking up the sport of table tennis, my Saturday mornings were spent at the Arima Tennis Court under the watchful eyes of my late coach, Mr. Byron. I eventually made a choice between these two racket sports and chose the green table.

My summer holidays (or August vacation as we call it in Trinidad and Tobago) were filled with car journeys with Tom. Tom was the guy my father entrusted with responsibility for picking me up from my family home and dropping me off at the table tennis camp. The camp was at the D'Abadie Community Centre during the summer months of the early 1990s.

In my early days playing at the Centre, Sherdon wasn't playing there yet, but his older brother was. However, Sherdon may very well have been busy peering into the Centre when I started playing there. Who knows? Apart from this, our families met and became close at church, and Sherdon became a long-time family friend.

The late Mr. Cecil James ran the club where the table tennis camps were held. After my first summer camp at the D'Abadie Youths Table Tennis Club, I continued to hone my table tennis skills at that club and later at the Woodbrook Gladiators Club, under the watchful eyes of Mr. Aubrey Edwards and Mrs. Verna Edwards (both of blessed memory).

The ebb and flow of my sports career

As a former national junior and university table tennis player, I competed in numerous competitions and won many accolades. My most notable achievements included the 2008 Caribbean Universities Sports Association Tournament Barbados (Most Disciplined Player, where I was last coached by the late Mrs. Verna Edwards); 2007 London Grand Prix Table Tennis Tournament (Quarterfinalist in Women's Band 2); 1997 Caribbean Junior Championships Puerto Rico (3rd place in teams); 1999 Charles Chocolates National Age Group Championships (1st place); 1999 Caribbean Junior Championships, Guyana (1st place in U-17 Teams) and being awarded the table tennis award at my high school, St. Joseph's Convent, Port-of-Spain, during the period 1997 to 1999.

Then there were the lows.

After being selected for one of my first overseas tournaments, I got my first taste of disappointment. It stemmed from administrative-related shortcomings when our tour to Curaçao had to be canceled because of a lack of funding. During my early touring days, I started encountering knee problems, which my sports doctor said I needed to resolve by strengthening the muscles around the knees with squats. While that provided some relief, I am not certain that this was the best or most holistic solution in the long term.

Faced with this challenge in a different country, I may have been presented with a wider range of solutions because I could have had access to a pool of different sports or medical specialists—like the athletes of today. In later years, insufficient corporate sponsorship thwarted my attempts at going to live and train in the United Kingdom.

Of all the sponsors I corresponded with, only one entity stepped forward with a cheque for the equivalent of approximately US$44–not even enough for a one-way plane ticket. In addition to that, in later years, the passing of one of my club coaches in the United Kingdom and three of my coaches in Trinidad and Tobago (Cecil James, Aubrey Edwards, and Verna Edwards) really jolted me.

Like the discipline and patriotism my father developed through being a Senior Cadet in high school, a level of patriotism develops in one's heart and soul when your country's Coat of Arms is emboldened with your country's name on your breastplate or the back of your T-shirt or track top. It is not only seared on this clothing, but it is seared on your heart. This happened to me. This caused the spark that ignited the eternal flame of my athlete's soul.

As such, no matter what I do; or how far I may travel from my country, (previously for competition; now for professional reasons) I always seek to represent not only myself but also my family and country with excellence.

Besides the patriotism and nationalism that representing my country at table tennis engendered, I also learned about discipline, respect, loyalty, strategy, teamwork, integrity, fair play, and being gracious in defeat.

I recall a period of unsatisfactory performance in local tournaments that devastated me. One afternoon, when I returned home from a tournament, to comfort me and lift my spirits, my mother, Patricia Barrow shared with me the biblical scripture, "I can do all things through Christ who strengthens me." (Phillipians 4:13). She told me to repeat this constantly in difficult moments. This scripture and all the lessons I have learned through sports have served and continue to serve me well in my personal and professional life.

At various times during my high school and university years, academics took center stage, and table tennis had to be placed on the back burner. It happened during my Caribbean Examinations Council (CXC)/General Certificate of Secondary Education (GCSE) O-Level and GCE Cambridge A-Level Exams. Academics had to be given priority in my home, so I had to forego any tours or tournaments during exam prep. One unforgettable training stint I had to relinquish was the opportunity to attend a table tennis training camp in the mecca of table tennis - China!

There is a critical window in which a local table tennis player would need to be immersed in advanced overseas training and competition to take their game to a higher level. I recognized this, and I expressed a desire to not do the final two years of my seven-year high school and instead seek a foreign-based sport or sport and academic scholarship where I could train and compete at a higher level in a more advanced country.

As none of my older siblings adopted this course with their education, my mother was not open to exercising this option with me, so I had to complete my high school education.

Early sports administration career

My first job after high school was in an administrative role for a zonal football association in Trinidad and Tobago in 2001. There I assisted the General Secretary with organizing various youth and adult competitions, prepared and issued press releases, registered players, and organized social events along with other administrative duties.

I also met my first work friend, now a medical doctor, who I share an over 21-year friendship with. She worked in another football organization that had offices in the same building. I also volunteered for events and assisted with fundraisers of the Trinidad & Tobago Table Tennis Association. When I was leaving my first post-high school sports role, one of my supervisors asked if I planned to pursue sports law, to which I said no. It's ironic how things would change years later!

The jealous mistress trumps

During my university studies for my first degree, at the University of the West Indies, in St. Augustine, Trinidad, I was able to get a minor amount of table tennis training to compete and represent my university. However, the academic demands of studying law at the University of the West Indies, Cavehill Campus, Barbados, and attending Hugh Wooding Law School, St. Augustine Trinidad, required that I prioritize my studies ahead of table tennis training or competition. So, I trained and competed much less than I did when I was pursuing my first degree, in high school, or furthermore, when I started playing the sport.

I have dedicated several years of my sporting life to the green table and reverted to the lawn tennis court occasionally during my law studies and as a form of leisurely exercise and a de-stressor. This was only when I didn't have access to regular table tennis when I worked as an associate attorney at a law firm in Antigua and Barbuda. During this time, I knew my competitive years in table tennis were inevitably drawing to a close. The demands of the "jealous mistress"—the law and the devotion to high-level table tennis training and competition just couldn't co-exist in my life.

In the same way that cricket would have undergone a revolution with the introduction of the T-20 and T-10 versions of the game, I have lived through the 2000s revolution of table tennis to make the sport more viable for televised viewers. For example, I have seen the size of the ball change, the length of the game change from twenty-one points (with each player having five serves) to eleven points (with each player having two serves), and the banning of concealing the ball when serving, among other changes to the game over the years.

These developments and the wear and tear on my knees and the wrist (of my playing hand) made playing and training more difficult. This was most apparent when I briefly returned to play in 2019 after returning from Antigua and Barbuda, and while training for a corporate tournament (pre-Covid-19) which was canceled after the declaration of the pandemic. I could no longer push my body to the lengths I did as a junior national player, where I would train for almost entire days at the Jean Pierre Complex or Woodbrook Youth Centre, Port-of-Spain.

That enduring gift

After practicing as an associate law firm attorney in both Trinidad and Tobago and Antigua and Barbuda and working as in-house counsel in Trinidad and Tobago, I started my solo legal practice in Trinidad and Tobago during Q4 2021.

After opening my practice, the following words stuck with me from a teaching I was listening to during the pandemic: "Your gifts will make a way for you; use them!" I consider my exposure to and involvement in sports to be one of those gifts. And, having been on the receiving end and witnessing poor sports governance over the years, I am a strong advocate and supporter of improved sports governance locally and regionally. I also long to see an improvement in corporate sponsorship, in all sports, which is still a challenge for local and Caribbean athletes to this day.

I have had a full-circle experience with sports, which has led to my decision to include sports as part of my legal and consulting service offerings, to collaborate with Sherdon for these services and to co-author this chapter, and join forces on other projects and initiatives, since we share a similar vision for the improvement of the industry.

"For me, sport is the greatest metaphor for real life."

—Sherdon Pierre

Peeking from the outside

My journey in sports began with peeking through the crease of the bedroom door in the early morning hours to spy on my grandfather as he watched sports. Not long after, I outsmarted him to be his company. The routine of a typical seven-year-old does not include waking up early hours of the morning before school to watch sports, but for my grandfather, it was part of holistic education. This is true because I vividly remember the many inspiring cricket innings by my hero Brian Charles Lara and the emotions I felt, and the lessons I learned on discipline and concentration.

From then onwards, it was a known fact that I was going to be involved in sports. It was embedded in me. I had significant support from my family. They appreciated the plethora of benefits sports provided as it also allowed me to follow my dreams, which were understandably blurred by the limited opportunities for a career in sport in Trinidad and Tobago and the wider Caribbean.

Being an inquisitive and adventurous youngster, I used to sneak out from home and peek through holes in the wall of the dilapidated D'Abadie Community Center to see my older brother play table tennis. I was exposed to various sports at different levels, but my true love was table tennis, after that timely introduction in July 1998.

The D'Abadie Youths Table Tennis Club operated from the Center, which was relatively close to where I lived. It was my hiding spot until the coach of the club, Cecil James, caught me. He invited me in with a racket on entry. I went from peeking from the outside into the reality of sports, and I owe him greatly for that opportunity.

He was from my area, went to my church, and was friends with my grandparents, so I literally couldn't get away from him. Mr. James became one of the greatest mentors of my life. He coached hundreds of children and produced the most national players in the country, all in good faith and in the spirit of volunteerism.

Even at a young age, I realized that an effective sporting system is far more important than the quality of sports facilities, but government officials seemed to think otherwise. Our training center was not in the best of conditions, but many national athletes were produced from this proven system since the 1970s, at this one facility. This is a prime example of utilizing what is available and trusting the process.

Practice, preparation, pride

Within two months of my introduction to the sport, I progressed quickly and took part in my first tournament. It was broadcasted on national television, and I placed third in the "Boys Under 10" category. The next day, pride lifted my head high and was evidenced by a broad permanent smile as I walked through the gates of my elementary school compound, Domine Private School. That added motivation inspired me to train even harder and to execute better.

I trained with the senior players at least three days per week whilst playing other sporting activities on the remaining days. I improved immensely because they were better than I was, and we did a lot of repetitive work, as our coaching method was not advanced, but we mastered the basics and made up the rest with soul and determination. There were so many talented players in the club that we had to be innovative to gain an edge over each other. It was survival of the fittest.

My dominance in the sport continued for several years nationally and regionally, as I toured throughout several regional and international countries (Guyana, Barbados, Puerto Rico, and the USA) and won medals. I was one of the few English-speaking Caribbean players to be given a standing ovation and media coverage in rival-playing nations.

At twelve years old, on the national junior team, one of my most notable achievements was being the first person from the region to ever be highlighted in one of the International Table Tennis Federation (ITTF) magazines by Dr. Chandra Madhosingh. He was a fellow Trinidadian who passed away in December 2022; he served on several international committees.

Sport as an academic option and the hurdle

In retrospect, at my high school, Trinity College East, I represented the institution in Athletics, Cricket, Football, Track & Field, and, of course, the Table-Tennis national team. Fulfilling all these activities enabled me to gain time management skills, develop managerial skills and harness the general competence to become the person I am today. It was my physical education teacher, Ken Andrew Marin, who encouraged me and guided me toward choosing sports as an academic option.

I knew I was at a crossroads, even though my parents were supportive of me pursuing my studies. I received partial scholarship offers from two universities in the US. That meant my parents would have to fund some of it, which I kept to myself and declined before they found out and thought of overextending themselves, especially having two other siblings with promise in sports.

Fortunately, I was offered a scholarship in Trinidad from the University of Trinidad and Tobago. I saw it as an opportunity to train in the comfort of home (where most of the team were clubmates) and show the world that the production of players can occur in our backyard. The program had several challenges, but we persevered. Then came the hurdle—an injury.

After several months of "playing through the pain," what I assumed was a muscle injury turned out to be an enlarged umbilical hernia that needed immediate attention. Psychologically, it was a disaster. I hated watching from the sidelines and being inactive for the first time in my life. I wasn't coping well physically and emotionally.

My grandmother, who was a pillar of strength and comfort in my life, persuaded me to postpone the surgery for a few weeks to prepare mentally for the transition. Little did I know she was going to die a few days later, adding to my already excruciating pain.

One month later, my surgery was eventually done, but the recovery process was prolonged. I was out for six months, missing my final year as a junior, which is crucial in transitioning to senior-level sports. At times, we see athletes returning from injuries and expect so much from them right away. There is rarely any emphasis on behind-the-scenes recovery, and if there was any, it would be on the physical rather than the mental.

With the joy of being back in the groove finally came an

unprescribed dose of sorrow months later. I was devastated when I was notified that I lost my scholarship via a text message a few days shy of my 19th birthday without a reasonable explanation. The reasons for this are still a mystery, yet to be solved. Questions are still to be answered after several podium finishes during that period. But I persevered.

For years I was letting my racket do the talking against adversities, This time, it was my pen. It was challenging to commute two hours to and from campus. My playing time decreased significantly, with the focus shifted to completing my bachelor's in sports studies degree. Once that was accomplished, I enrolled the following semester to pursue an international master's in sport for development, which was a tremendous challenge. I finally completed it years later, with the timely intervention of a dedicated and patient supervisor.

Trust your gut feelings

I was fortunate to get an internship at the TT Pro League, which was the office of the professional football (soccer) league. My portfolio was the assistant secretary to an inspirational and empowering boss, Julia Baptiste.

My focus was overseeing the youth League, sending information to the media, registering players, liaising with Fédération Internationale de Football Association (FIFA), and organizing for match days. It was an excellent experience as we - two former classmates - were given the opportunity to be creative within the league, which was struggling in attendance at matches and with sponsors.

It was a weekend trip with my best friend, Imtiaz Mohammed, to witness T&T win the last-ever edition of the Caribbean Cricket Championship in St. Lucia. It was a gut feeling that made me agree as it was literally the last of my savings spent, and we had promised each other that we would travel to watch whenever our national team was in a final.

He was the person who encouraged me to manage athletes. However, upon returning from my spontaneous trip, I was regrettably informed that my job had become redundant. Distraught, I remember the exact words when I relayed this news to my mom: "Come home, you got a roof over your head, and you wouldn't starve for food."

When I thought that was the only life-altering moment, Imtiaz died in a car accident two months later at age twenty-two. Sometimes, you must trust that gut feeling! It cost me my savings, but I received a lifetime of memories.

Invest in yourself

In the latter part of 2013, I decided to invest in myself, hoping it would pay dividends for years to come. I looked for educational opportunities via conferences and workshops to boost my knowledge. What can only be described as divine intervention happened; I was recommended by Caribbean Youth Advocate, Dr. Henry Charles to attend a Human Rights Conference in the Bahamas.

After participating, I was able to better understand the key values in society, how to interact with others, and strategies to deal with certain uncommon situations. This venture was made possible through several fundraisers from my family and friends and my stingy savings.

My former professor and motivator, Jay Mafukidze, insisted that I represented the Caribbean region at the Olympic For Humanity conference in Olympia, Greece, in 2013. At the conference, I was taught how to design an effective program, as well as the steps required to monitor and evaluate it. When I returned home, I took some time to design the program, and after careful consideration, I submitted it for funding, only to be told that it was unusable and irrelevant! Surprisingly enough, two years later, a similar program was launched with just a tweak of the name. I learned a significant lesson in copyright infringement. Well, at least I hope the kids benefited.

In the Caribbean, some are still seeing sport as a co-extracurricular activity and are not seeing its great importance in society. At the EducaSport World Forum in Paris, France (in 2013), I learned how to merge education and sports programs into one curriculum. There are far more similarities than differences between the two of them. I was exposed to several academies, including Tottenham Hotspur FC, an English Premier League team.

The International Youth Forum in Russia (in 2014) was one of the greatest experiences in my life, being around so many like-minded people of my age from different parts of the world. I was selected to present the culture of my country to over 150 countries and 5,000 people. What did I use to highlight us? Sports and entertainment!

Self-gain is cheap but...expensive!

Political interference eschews the harness of development in the sport. There is nothing new to this side of the coin. You never know how things will unfold off the court and more so at the level of administration. Many issues that affect the athlete are left at the mercy of decision-makers to the detriment of the active player. I became sensitized to this after being unfairly treated on several occasions.

Administrators seem to thrive on schadenfreude and will bicker about minor issues, and while this was occurring, our standards were falling farther behind compared to our international rivals. This surely was a deterrent, and the focus wasn't on the gap between us and our rivals but on personal agendas and selfishness. For improvement to exist, one must be selfless and have the desire to see the development of others over personal gain.

"Dream Big, Work Hard, Stay Focused, and Surround Yourself with Good People"[1]

In order to put my knowledge and experience to the test of being a sports practitioner, I registered my company, Ehlam Ma'aya Management (translated as "Dream with Me," in Arabic), which was later changed to "In for More Sport Agency" (IFM) in memory of my best friend, Imtiaz. It was necessary because the athletes of the Caribbean needed proper representation on and off the field. It's a tough task, and the odds are stacked heavily against me because most of the sports are held outside of the Caribbean region, but networking is essential.

---

1 Facebook post by Imtiaz Mohammed in 2013.

We need more charismatic individuals to bridge the problematic gap athletes face who are transitioning from junior to senior and amateur to professional. I have gathered academic qualifications and experience, and I'm passionate and ready to take that leap!

I have been a sports journalist for the last seven years, taught life skills and sports at an after-school program, co-hosted sports radio shows, and managed athletes and sports teams, which has been my most enjoyable accomplishment.

Over the years, I have volunteered at over fifteen organizations in various capacities throughout the Caribbean. My motivation is to relish seeing the progress of others, whether in sports or other areas. Not everyone will become the next top athlete or have the best-paying job, but you can ensure that they are well-rounded individuals, which will, in return, lead to a better society. Imagine the exhilarating feeling of cheering on an athlete you developed at the Olympic Games or hearing a song on the radio from a former participant in your program.

My passion still exists for the sport of table tennis even though I'm a recreational player who plays a few competitions in between. The devotion is now beyond the playing arena and in helping the upcoming generation progress further than I did.

Sometimes, I sit and wonder what could have been if my path had progressed differently. At least, I live out my boyhood dreams of being a professional athlete through the eyes and experiences of the internationally renowned athletes who I have very close relationships with. It is something I hold in high esteem because the questions to them are detailed and plentiful, but grateful that they endure my consistent pestering.

I have had magnificent encounters working in sports. The camaraderie, heartwarming feeling of suiting up in national colors, or seeing your flag blow in the wind on top of the winning podium. However, as with everything, the struggles and the frustration are plentiful.

As the joke goes, "Sports people are always the ones to be paid last or have their price negotiated." My grandmother prayed nightly that I would get a good office job; this prayer is now repeated by my mother. They know well that the active genes inherited by my ancestors cannot sit behind a desk because I was born to be outdoors.

Resilience, discipline, patience, respect, and teamwork are some personality traits that I have learned and endured to truly understand what the soul of an athlete is.

In life, you need to have faith to be gifted with fate! That is the only way I can explain reconnecting with Bellina, who I have known for almost my entire life. We represented the same table tennis club - D'Abadie Youths Table Tennis Club and attended the same church. Now, we share one common vision and have lots of plans, starting with this co-authored chapter.

We will continue to share our personal and professional experiences in the sports industry, both individually and collaboratively, as we bring our vision for the improvement of the industry, our country, Trinidad and Tobago, and the Caribbean region to life!

ABOUT BELLINA

Bellina Barrow is a Trinidad and Tobago national and the principal attorney at Tenoreque Legal, which is a law practice that she founded during Q4 2021. She is also a co-author of the anthology Women in Law: Discovering the True Meaning of Success (Ramses House, 2022), along with further legal and other articles.

She is a law graduate of Hugh Wooding Law School, Trinidad, 2012, and the University of the West Indies, Cave Hill Campus (Barbados), 2010. She also holds a BSc in government with minors in human resource management and management information systems from the University of the West Indies, St. Augustine Campus (Trinidad), which she earned in 2005. She was admitted to legal practice in Trinidad and Tobago in 2012, in Antigua and Barbuda in 2014 and in the British Virgin Islands in 2023. Before her legal career, she was a human resources professional in Trinidad and Tobago and in the United Kingdom.

She has previous local and Caribbean law firm experience and corporate in-house counsel experience in the Trinidad and Tobago financial services sector. At Tenoreque Legal, she focuses her practice on civil, commercial/corporate law (inclusive of cross-border and commercial arbitration disputes and fintech), public and employment law and she also offers sports law and other sports-related and human resource services.

You can follow her on LinkedIn, via www.tenorequelegalandconsulting.com; or contact her via info@tenorequelegalandconsulting.com.

ABOUT SHERDON

Sherdon Pierre is a sports enthusiast from birth and is a former national table tennis player for Trinidad and Tobago.

He attained his bachelor's in sport studies (2008–2011) and graduated with his international master's in sport for development in 2017 at the University of Trinidad and Tobago after attaining a sports scholarship.

He wears many hats in bettering and empowering his community in Trinidad and Tobago as he is the president of the D'Abadie Youths Table Tennis Club, president of Talk Tsu Toastmasters Club, member of the D'Abadie Lions Club, vice president of the D'Abadie Community Council, assistant secretary of the D'Abadie Progressive Athletics Club, and a former executive of the Trinidad & Tobago Table Tennis Association (2017–2019).

He is the first person from the Caribbean region to be elected to the Media Committee of the International Table Tennis Federation in November 2021.

He has been a sports journalist for almost a decade with over 600 articles inclusive of features, leading stories and overseas assignments. He is a budding sports agent/manager and established the "In For More Sports Agency" in 2022 to promote the athletes of the Caribbean to the wider world in various sports. He manages several athletes across the Caribbean in different sports and aims to grow in the future.

He has performed the role of media manager for teams for Table-Tennis (2018), Volleyball (2019 and 2020), and Cricket (2019 and in 2022 winning the Trinidad Dream XI T-10 cricket tournament with the Blue Devils team).

In 2023 Sherdon became an ambassador for clothing company Unique Society Apparel based in the Caribbean.

He is a true community practitioner as he works assiduously to build a better tomorrow.

Connect with In For More Sports Agency at www.informoresports.com, ifmsportsagency on Instagram and IFM Sports Agency on Facebook.

PART II

ADVICE FOR THE TRANSITION AWAY FROM SPORT

CHAPTER 8

FORMER ATHLETES' HEROIC JOURNEYS AND DREAMS

BY JOHN O'BRIEN

J im Taylor and Bruce Ogilvie, who are both academics and sports psychologists, invented a framework in 1994 to help understand the journey of retirement from sports. From the beginning, they made a box labeled "Causes of athletic retirement: age, deselection, injury, free choice." When I read about their conceptual model while doing doctoral research for my dissertation, my jaw dropped.

I was already seven years "retired" from sports. Soccer was my sport, and I was pretty good when I played, though I was not on the field very often! In my athletic career, I made it to the top European platform representing Ajax of Amsterdam and winning Dutch titles while playing in the esteemed Champions league. I represented my country, the good old US of A, at both the Olympics and twice in the World Cup - on one occasion, as a quarterfinalist.

I exchanged brief spells of full fitness with lengthy injury periods spent on the massage table or watching games from the stands. So much so that at the tender age of twenty-nine, when many pros are in their prime, I called it quits.

So, what was it about the aforementioned article that made my jaw drop? It was the realization that each athlete's transition from sports differs and that my experience need not fit with those of others.

My misfortune placed me firmly in the injury camp, with a potential deselection right around the corner. After spending four years trading off injury for injury, I had lost hope. The cause of my athletic retirement was not a single career-ending injury but an accumulation of injuries, leaving me frustrated, fearful, searching for hope, and with a severely reduced contract offer on the table. I decided not to take it, instead wanting to train on my own and see if I could get back to full fitness. Full fitness never came, and gradually I started training less and finding other things more interesting to do.

Several years passed before I realized that I would never play pro again. So, I had a small soccer retirement party where I brought out all my old jerseys and ones I had traded for. I invited some friends from my early soccer days and a couple of ex-pros, and we played one last time. We played to commemorate my heroic journey from an enthusiastic, young kid to an accomplished professional. After the party, I packed up the jerseys in a suitcase and put them in a basement, out of the way.

That retirement party, along with letting the Contractspelers Fonds KNVB (CFK), which oversaw pensions for all professional soccer players in the Netherlands, know that I was officially retired and would like my "bridging pension" to begin, were big markers in an adjustment process that has taken years. A bridging pension is a pension for a select amount of time (in my case, it was ten years from my retirement date) that provides financial support while the athlete transitions into a new career.

Seven years after my last pro game, and in my first year of my clinical psychology doctorate program, I was asked to research whatever was of interest to me. I wanted to know what in the world I had just been through, whether others were thinking about it, and how they were thinking about it. Taylor and Ogilvie's objective and succinct model gave the inquiry some structure, but now I want to get to the more personal parts.

Attachments and breakups

What if a sport was your lover? A meaningful, intimate relationship from which you receive satisfaction and contentment? A give-and-take with some general rules of engagement? It is not too far-fetched to think in these terms. In fact, sports psychologist, Tom Ferraro, building on Phyllis Greenacre's theory about gifted children, states that athletes who compete at a young age often transfer their interpersonal attachments to their sport and become tied to it in a serious way (2021).

The transition out of sports, thus, can be seen as a breakup. It is a time of rearranging bonds of attachment, and this is often accompanied by grief, anxiety, and all the individual ways we defend against emotional pain.

For me, this theory fits. I went through a painful breakup with an ex-lover just before my relationship with soccer was renegotiated, and the parallels are striking. At first, she acted in ways that communicated the relationship was ending, but I took protective measures and ended it first. This was similar to soccer because I rejected the diminished contract, possibly sensing that rejection was right around the corner. I needed to protect myself, and in those instances, I did.

After the relationships ended, I pretended I was fine but found myself intensely nervous when around both my ex and the pro soccer environment. I was hyper-aware of the relationship. In attending a pro game, I would wonder how I would be accepted. Might there still be some rejection? Might jealousy arise as soccer's attention is turned elsewhere and I am forgotten? In both of these instances, my self-worth was as fragile as glass, and I feared it would break and leave me in pieces.

Now, this is my reaction to a breakup, and it says a lot about me, my sensitive areas, and my psychological makeup. Others may have different reactions. In my research, I have seen many accounts of blaming the sport.

To be fair, sports are made up of imperfect humans vulnerable to subjectivity and societal ills like discrimination, sexism, homophobia, and racism. It takes a continual effort to improve our systems to make them more equitable. Absolutely, there can be fault with the system. When I hear blaming and adopting a victim mentality, I often wonder if that could be a protective measure, protecting oneself from the pain of rejection. Or maybe it could be the worthlessness one may feel if the relationship ended because one's skill set was not matching the needs of the other.

Lastly, like a relationship, the seduction of sex with the ex, and returning to intimacy lingered after the relationship ended.

I could easily be swept into reverie when looking at old jerseys or artifacts. This could be seen as an engagement with and remembrance of that relationship—a relationship that had been both meaningful and painful and has taken a lot of time to find peace with.

Love and the insider/outsider dynamic

In my ongoing research of former athletes' dreams, I have been fortunate enough to hear stories about the bonds of attachment—dare I say, love:

Former pro:

"I dreamt I was on a professional MLS team that I had never played on, but with old teammates from different teams. We were at a youth tournament field and getting ready to practice. As I entered the soccer pitch, one character in the dream called my name and said, 'What's up?' in a welcoming way. I started putting my cleats on."

"It was as if he had his arms wide open and was welcoming me," the dreamer shared. The dreamer described having warm, comforting, and positive feelings in the dream.

Former national team player:

"I dreamt I got recalled to the US team as a player. It was about a year after I had retired, and we were at a domestic camp. The coach said, 'You've done a great job, welcome back!' I took my stuff (cleats, shin guards, etc.) to the bench to get ready."

A third retired pro:

"I dreamt I was in a diner with a handful of ex-teammates who I liked and who were all from different teams and different parts of my career. We were discussing events going on with our former teams and preparing for a future alumni event of some sort."

He described a general feeling of warmth and affection for each of the teammates at the diner.

Building on the idea of one's sport being like a lover, these dreams show both how impactful acceptance is, and how powerful rejection is. Are we together? Am I in, or am I not? These are often the questions looming over aspiring athletes' heads as they climb the ranks.

For me, the ins were making it to the pros, getting invited to the national team, and appearing on the World Cup roster. All of these were thresholds of significant meaning for outlining the terms of my relationship with soccer. I was in! My first professional contract and the epic team picture at the beginning of the season both symbolically formalized our relationship and proved that we were together. Other teammates may have been rejected and moved outside the relationship.

The physical spaces people have access to around the stadium depict the rules of the relationship. If you are on the inside, you are in skyboxes and locker rooms, while those rejected athletes have access to a seat number, concessions, and curated fan zones. Do they stop you at the front door or welcome you into the living room? Do you even share a bed? These are all varying levels of intimacy.

For many athletes, the accepted/rejected or insider/outsider aspect becomes a source of pride or shame and anger. If you ask an athlete what they miss about their sport, most often they will say it is the experience in the locker room. This is the place that symbolically serves the most intimacy, where one is clearly in the group and building bonds with others in the group.

With retirement, the relationship between the sport and the people in the sport changes. Breakups can happen in different ways, and new rules of the relationship are negotiated. Using this model, it is understandable that the transition out of sports can be painful, but in addition, there are other perspectives. Let's take a look at a developmental perspective.

Developmental framework

A developmental view, as it sounds, embraces the idea of the individual developing over time through certain general phases. Being an elite athlete involves serious dedication to a competitive environment at a young age. Usually, it ends in the twenties or thirties before the athlete has even made it to midlife. Erik Erikson's stages of psychosocial development name this time of likely retirement from sports as the sixth stage of individual development: intimacy vs isolation. Huh, sound familiar, sports lover?

The developmental perspective, and psychological theories in general, allow individuals to take a step back from their subjective self and see themselves more objectively as if looking down on their life from above. This practice is often relieving for clients, offering an "aha" moment regarding what they are going through. What usually follows is more calmness, acceptance of hard feelings, kindness towards one's self, and a better vantage point to make decisions.

Two developmental theories I like are Carl Jung and his idea of the self-growth process of individuation, and Joseph Campbell's "Hero's Journey." With Jung, individuation is the process of becoming more of one's self by integrating unconscious aspects of one's experience, while shedding the socially constructed persona.

In my transition from sports, I was able to relate to the process of shedding one's persona and fearfully stepping into a more authentic or individuated way of being. Here is a piece I later wrote about an experience I had while in the most tumultuous time of the transition.

"So, I moved on. And it was terrifying, and yet kind of thrilling in an adventurous sort of way. It was total self-dissolution. The persona I had constructed was no longer relevant. I sold my house in Amsterdam and said goodbye to friends in a serious way. All these bits that were my life through my twenties, my people, my purpose, and my routines, dissolved.

"Who was I socially? I used to receive validation weekly, if not daily, of my soccer specialness, a validation that lifted me up. Maybe it was a crutch. If not, at least an attachment. What would have happened if that specialness weren't there? I knew I would fall, but where to? A black hole, depression, self-loathing, catatonia?

"I remember driving down a bare, wide-cracked, concrete road in LA—dull, gray colors, chipped and worn yellow-and-white stripes, manufactured equidistant palms framing the road. This is strange, I thought. Is life absurd, or unreal? What's the meaning of all this? And suddenly, boom—vertigo!

"I no longer knew where my body ended and the world began. My breath grew shallow and rapid, my heart beat wildly, and the ground turned to liquid. But I managed to keep driving. The sensations were just short of a panic attack—luckily a good way from a psychotic breakdown.

"At that moment it seemed the training wheels of life, the soccer routine I had been attached to for seventeen years, literally since childhood: practice, sleep, eat, drink, recover, perform, just fell off. I looked up, my hands were still on the wheel, and I was still moving forward. Outside the weather was pleasant, 72 degrees, and the sky, the sky was cloudless. I did not know what was ahead and that was scary, but I knew things would be different from before and that was exciting."

I was not in Jungian analysis at the time, but Jung's developmental path would have had me engaging with unconscious aspects for guidance toward individuation: dreams, projections, feelings, and creative endeavors. In some ways, I was on a normal human developmental path. I was experiencing what many others have, just ramped up by the whole early sports retirement thing.

Next is Joseph Campbell, who came later and is most famous for his formative impact on George Lucas and his creation of the *Star Wars* series. Campbell outlined the heroic journey (see image), which has since become a template used in many creative writing stories. It is a metaphor for personal change where the protagonist (insert Luke Skywalker) sets off into the unknown, receives mentorship, experiences struggles, is changed in some way, and then returns with something valuable (for example, the capacity to use the force for good).

The athletic journey itself can be heroic, but I like to think of the moment an athlete decides to retire also as the start of a heroic journey. It is like Luke Skywalker on the precipice, returning to his farm on Tatooine, relinquishing his potential as a Jedi Knight or heeding the call, undergoing difficult training to better know himself, develop his skills and lead the rebel army.

In Campbell's book *The Hero with a Thousand Faces*, he says, "The usual hero adventure begins with someone from whom something has been taken... The person then takes off on a series of adventures beyond the ordinary, either to recover what has been lost or to discover some life-giving elixir." This can be the transformational process of the retiring athlete and may include struggles, depression, as well as hard-earned skills or wisdom.

The hero can heed the call or initially refuse the call and instead walk away. Here is the dream of a former aspiring pro golfer, right on the cutline of making it or not, early in his career and considering stopping:

> "I hit the ball over a small hill, follow it, and see it has gone into an outhouse. Three Hells Angels are standing by the door ominously. They say it went in there as if daring me to go get it. I abandon the ball and walk away."

Dreams, like the developmental path, often show the dreamer something new. The dreamer is faced with an obstacle in the way of retrieving his golf ball - ominous and hellacious gangsters - and he decides to abandon it. Years later, reflecting on the dream material he shared, he did feel like, at that time, there were psychological obstacles of frustration and low self-esteem holding him back from being a successful pro. He chose to walk away from the professional career path and get a job in the golf industry. The time and conditions were not right for him to face that adventure and challenge of his own angelic and demonic (Hell's Angels reference) psychological blocks.

Erikson, Jung, and Campbell outline stages and paths of normal human development over a lifespan. The athlete's transition out of sports lands right on top of this predictable human trajectory. And now from theories rooted in time, let us look at the timeless impact of sports on the deepest parts of one's being.

The timeless impact of sports and the never-changing "I"

Ask an eighty-year-old if they are different from when they were twenty. Amid the many possible responses about the body changes and life experiences, almost all will say they still feel like the same person. Our "I" does not change. And for most athletes, the sport experience is part of that "I."

I started researching former athletes' dreams of their sport because I was astonished by my own sports dreams. Fifteen years after my last competitive match, I would wake up in my dream in another part of the world, getting ready to go to a stadium with my teammates. People I used to work with and had not spoken to for years, former teammates and coaches would appear, and we would interact or play. I would either find myself struggling in a game or pulling off great moves. This occurred even though I was no longer in the soccer industry and was only playing the sport periodically.

I needed to know that I was not alone in having these dreams, and I found out I am not. The twenty participants in the research study, 0–30 years out of their sport also experienced positive, negative, joyful, and distressful sport-related dreams.

One dreamer, whose sports career stopped short of making it to the elite level in basketball, describes having many positive dreams of sports. In a recent dream, thirty years after playing competitively, he jumped and just kept going up almost as if he could fly. He described it as a wonderful experience, though somewhat disappointing when he awoke and recognized that his fifty-year-old body was incapable of transcendent flight.

Sport is a physical endeavor as well as a captivating, metaphorical one. Elation and hope are physical experiences impacting the athlete in deep biological ways, metaphorically captivating sports fans across the globe.

The most common dream former athletes experienced was that of performance anxiety. At night while sleeping, anxiety would arise, transforming their bodies from peace to a state of fight, flight, or freeze, accompanied by tense muscles, sweat, and a rapid pulse. Here are some dreams of former players:

"In my soccer dreams I'm missing a piece of equipment, or I'm hindered in getting to the fields in some way. I'm always a player and I'm always trying to get to a game or field, and something causes me to be late or unable to play."

"I have a reoccurring dream that I have about twice a year. In this dream I am playing with the national team, so everyone is very intense and very focused. The game is about to start, and I am trying to tie my cleats but just can't tie them. I am rushing, but in my dream, I can't tie them."

"I have a dream sometimes that I am at a World Cup Qualifier with the U.S. National Team, and the head coach is telling me to get ready to sub-in, and I can't get my 'soccer socks' on to sub-in. He keeps calling to me and says it is time, 'I need you now.'"

The biological experience of fear for these athletes is all the same, but they all have slightly different stories in their dreams. One experiences tight socks as the obstacle, and associates this with nervous memories of childhood, trying to hurry to put on tight socks and catch up with his older siblings; a horrible feeling of fear of being left out or left behind.

For another, people become the obstacles, which leads the discussion down the path of if the former athlete has different parts of themselves that are sometimes in conflict and want different things. The athlete resonates with the experience of feeling sabotaged by a part of themselves that works against their best intentions.

In psychotherapy, the goal would be to further understand these parts of oneself, which could start with doing what Jung called an active imagination with the dream figure, where one dialogues with it in your imagination to find out what they value and are protecting. In this way, the athlete, like the person, is on a developmental trajectory of individuation, growing more into themselves, and gradually making what is unconscious conscious.

The physical nature of sports and the metaphor of sports reach deep into the bodies and minds of dedicated practitioners, impacting the way we make sense of the outer world and our own experience. For former athletes, the use of the sport setting in their dreams is, in a way, unsurprising. It is a familiar base to call upon to help process one's own experience.

For me and the participants in the dream research, sports was a very mixed experience, one of enormous difficulty, sacrifice, and pain, and also wonderful elation, pleasure, and pride. Engagement in elite sports required discipline of the mind and body, regularity, and routine.

Life after sports is a whole different encounter. It challenges the individual to grow in new ways. In post-sports life, the affectionate gaze of an admiring public lessens or, for some athletes, evaporates completely. This can make the second phase, life after sports, seem less important. However, as a person and as a psychology candidate, I find the next phase to be the most beautiful. Dormant desires bubble up from some unknown place, personalities change and strengthen, and the struggle and pain of making one's way, if managed well, creates a deepening empathy for others, a steadier hand, and a depth of character.

Making space for oneself to heal from the loss of a lover or to grow by allowing space for some inner guide can be deeply rewarding, and in line with, as Jung calls it, one's purpose in life: individuating.

References

Campbell, J. (2012). The hero with a thousand faces (3rd ed.). New World Library.

Ferraro, T. (2021, August 31). Our Town: Giftedness a blessing or a curse. The Island 360. https://theisland360.com/opinions-100/our-town-giftedness-a-blessing-or-a-curse/

ABOUT JOHN

Dr. John O'Brien is an accomplished individual with a remarkable background in both sports and psychology. As a former elite soccer player, he represented the United States in two World Cups and the Olympics while also playing for the prestigious Ajax of Amsterdam. His extensive experience in sports has provided him with a unique perspective on the psychological and social factors that affect athletes.

In addition to his sporting achievements, Dr. O'Brien is a practicing psychotherapist with a doctorate in psychology, making him an expert in the bio-psycho-social aspects of mental health. He has an impressive track record of helping people overcome life's challenges through his work as a mental skills coach for Division I College Athletes, athlete advocacy through the U.S. Soccer Athlete Council, and sports-based youth development with Soccer Without Borders.

Dr. O'Brien's expertise in athlete retirement led to his development of a workshop that addresses the social-emotional challenges faced by athletes when they retire from sport. This led to consulting with Major League Soccer about their athlete transition programs, which is a testament to his contribution to the field.

Despite his many professional achievements, Dr. O'Brien values his personal relationships above all else. He notes his biggest achievements as being in a committed, intimate, and vulnerable relationship with his wife, having more authentic relationships with his friends and family and being an engaged father of two children.

To learn more about Dr. John O'Brien's professional services and interests, you can visit his websites at www.johnobrienpsyd.com or www.johnobriensportpsych.com. His unique blend of expertise in sports and psychology makes him an exceptional resource for anyone seeking support for their mental and emotional well-being.

CHAPTER 9

TRANSITIONS AND MENTAL HEALTH

BY BETH LORELL

I wasn't an elite competitor. I never qualified for an event or won any titles. But I was always serious about sports. My first love was running. I completed many events where I started and finished with the masses; however, no podium finishes or standout performances. But I trained, and I loved it. Then I discovered cycling, and my life changed.

I would spend many hours a week on my bike. Mornings, evenings, weekdays, and weekends. Although I'm not a morning person, I would wake up at 4:30 so I could ride before work. I joined a cycling club and dabbled in racing. I brought my bike with me on weekends away and took one-to-two-week annual summer vacations with 60–100 miles of riding per day.

I was not a remarkable cyclist, but I worked hard at it, and I held my own. Cycling was a core component of my routine. I would get home from my daily rides to messages saying, "Hey, Beth, you're probably still riding. Call me when you get home."

I rode my bike. That's what I did. And everyone knew it. Cycling took up a lot of my time, and it was a huge part of my identity.

Before I tell you about my transition out of cycling, I'm going to talk about transitioning out of sport with special attention to mental health. I hope you come away from this with some new perspectives on transitioning and some tips on how to approach transitions, related or unrelated to sport.

No health without mental health

"There is no health without mental health," says the World Health Organization (WHO).[2] Mental health is part of the vast network of systems that affects our overall health and functioning. It is linked to physical health, recovery from illness and injury, meaningful relationships, and healthy behaviors, among other factors that impact health and quality of life.

Mental health, like physical health, fluctuates. We can feel physically fit one day and get a cold or cough the next. We can feel joy in one moment and heartache and pain the next.

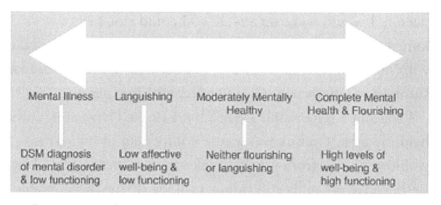

Bridget Norsworthy

---

2 World Health Organization. (n.d.). *Promoting mental health.* Retrieved September 7, 2022, from https://www.who.int/westernpacific/activities/promoting-mental-health

Mental health moves along a continuum, where there are shades of both well and unwell mental health. We each have a uniquely contoured psyche that contributes to how we think, feel, and behave in different situations. A range of emotional experiences is natural. It's human.

Transitions and mental health

Transitioning out of sport can be an intense experience that affects our movement along the mental health continuum. Some transitions occur organically and naturally, without effort. Others occur with intention and planning. Still, others are jolting and unsettling. Transitions are nuanced, and each experience is unique to the individual going through it.

There are five themes I see as central to transitioning out of sport and apply to transitions in general:

1. Loss
2. Acceptance
3. Identity Modification
4. Adjustment
5. Transition Planning

These phases are not linear. We might move through them one at a time or go through them concurrently. We even repeat phases. There is no universal way to experience transition.

Loss

Transition is change, and change is loss. Every change, even positive change, involves loss. We experience loss when we part with something. When athletes transition out of sport, they experience the loss of many things. Here are some examples:

- Teammates
- Coaches
- Training regimen
- Daily structure
- Thrill of competition
- Identity as an athlete (more on this coming up)
- Support network
- Sport community

Upon transitioning out of sport, athletes may also lose their sense of purpose and self-worth. When people leave their sport without fulfilling the goals they set out to achieve—because retirement came earlier than expected or their career didn't play out the way they imagined—they experience a loss of their vision. They lose the future they pictured for themselves.

With loss comes grief. Grief is the acute pain that follows a loss. It's a natural response that can generate a range of emotions: sadness, loneliness, regret, worry, shock, and anger. There is more than one way to experience grief, and it's important to allow ourselves the time and permission to grieve in our own way. Grief is not comfortable, but it is unavoidable. When we internalize our emotions instead of expressing them, a battle ensues within and mental health can suffer.

Imagine you're pushing a beach ball underwater. It takes a lot of force to hold it down, and the ball is pushing back up at you.

It's a battle between you and the ball, and the ball always wins. You can only hold it down for so long before it pops up.

The same thing happens with our emotions. It takes a tremendous amount of effort to push our emotions down. We fight to push our emotions down, but they ultimately surface.

One simple change can alter the entire experience. For instance, if you lift the beach ball above the water instead of pushing it down, the ball feels lighter. When we face our emotions and let ourselves notice them—when we lift them above the surface, like the beach ball—they feel lighter. We can then release them and make room for new emotions and experiences.

The potent emotions that often accompany grief and loss can be tough to handle. Let them rise above the surface. In the same way that many athletes rely on teammates and coaches, now too is the time to lean on others. Ask for help. There is no trophy for going at it alone.

Acceptance

Transitioning out of sport can be difficult, especially when the transition is not by choice. Acceptance is more than a statement saying, "Yes, I know this happened," or "I accept that it's out of my control." Genuine acceptance is making those statements but without the inner voice that often dwells on how much you dislike the situation or how much you wish things were different.

That internal chatter will happen, and that's natural. But to achieve true acceptance, we must move beyond the dialogue that's fighting against what's happening. Acceptance doesn't mean we like the situation. It means we recognize we cannot change it, and we disengage from the battle against it.

My internal dialogue was brutal before I accepted my exit from cycling. *I'm so weak. I should have the physical and mental strength to persist and push through this. What's wrong with me?* I fought against nature instead of embracing it. It took some time for me to realize that the changes coming upon me were beyond my control and could not be wished away.

Even when we cannot change our circumstances, we can change how we feel by creating a new mindset and developing a new perspective. Instead of focusing on what was lost, focus on what could be. Rather than staring at a door that has closed, consider what's on the other side. Imagine the possibilities for yourself. Visualize your dream scenario. Even if the full picture isn't realistic, a piece of it could be.

I struggled to envision a satisfying routine without cycling. However, I detected an inkling of relief from the idea that I'd have a later start to my day and more free time in my week. I wasn't sure what I'd do with the time, but the idea of gaining extra hours was appealing and softened the edges of this rough spot.

Achieving acceptance takes effort, but over time, resilience grows, and movement through transition becomes more peaceful. Acceptance frees up energy and mind space for us to see our situation through a different lens—a lens that magnifies parts of ourselves we may never have seen before.

Identity modification

For serious athletes, performance is the defining factor for most of their lives. The dedication required to excel at an elite level leaves limited time for anything else. Athletic performance and connection with sport are key contributors to an athlete's sense of pride and self-worth.

It makes sense that one's identity is closely tied to something that person has devoted years to developing and sharpening. It becomes harmful when a person sees their value and identity as dependent on their performance in sport and believes their only purpose is to excel in that one area.

This is *identity foreclosure*—when a person commits to one singular identity without fully exploring other options.[3] When a person's sole purpose in life is sport, the transition out can shatter their sense of identity: "Who am I without my sport?" Athletes often struggle to answer that question.

For many people, what they do is who they are. While it's understandable how this frame of mind can develop, it doesn't have to be this way. We are all more than one thing. We can have diverse purposes that don't interfere with each other. An athlete can be an elite performer and pursue other interests. When we are well-rounded and devote ourselves to more than one purpose, we become more interesting. Life becomes more interesting. Having a variety of interests and roles in life doesn't inevitably dilute the focus on sport performance. Research

---

3 Brewer, B. W., & Petitpas, A. J. (2017). Athletic identity foreclosure. *Current Opinion in Psychology, 16*, 118–122. https://doi.org/10.1016/j.copsyc.2017.05.004.

suggests that involvement in pre-retirement planning can boost performance and the length of an athlete's career.[4]

A person can have a strong athletic identity without having an exclusive athletic identity. A person can be dedicated to their sport while spending time doing other things they enjoy. A well-rounded identity is a valuable asset. It's like having a diversified financial portfolio. You are investing in yourself, and you create a healthier future when you partake in a variety of interests in your life. This also builds confidence and purpose, which can serve you well in and out of sport.

Retiring from sport doesn't mean you need to retire your athletic identity. You don't have to give that up completely. It will always be a part of who you are. You don't lose your identity; you modify it. All the experiences accumulated during your athletic career continue to exist even as you develop other parts of yourself.

Our identities are not fixed. They naturally transform throughout life. We can move through change more easily when we see ourselves as flexible and realize that change is a part of living.

Adjustment

Adjustment is the action phase of a transition. This is when we take the reins and reclaim a sense of control over our lives. We realize we are more than an athlete, a retired athlete, or an injured athlete. This is the point when we put our ideas into motion. The possibilities that exist beyond sport become tangible, and a new

---

4 David Lavallee (2019) Engagement in Sport Career Transition Planning Enhances Performance, *Journal of Loss and Trauma*, 24:1, 1–8, DOI: 10.1080/15325024.2018.1516916.

vision for our life emerges. When a person allows their identity and self-worth to be connected with something other than sport, they experience a more fulfilling present and a higher-quality transition.

This is a very different way of life for a person who is used to a more programmed routine. Adjusting to life without a firm schedule can feel overwhelming. Unstructured day after unstructured day can roll into weeks and months. While it initially might feel nice to have an open schedule, after some time, people can feel aimless.

It doesn't have to be that way. Begin by considering what features of your sport inspired you and brought you joy. Look for those things in other places. You can't have your sport, but what did you love about it and where else can you find that?

Choose a few key activities to incorporate into your daily routine, such as exercise and connecting with other people to socialize and network. You may not see these early pursuits as direct connections to a job opportunity or career. The important point of this phase is to stay active in body and mind. Every conversation is another step that propels you further along in your journey.

Starting is often the hardest part, so keep it simple. Add one activity at a time and build from there. Your motivation might not be there yet. That's okay. Motivation isn't a prerequisite for action. It often comes after you begin an activity or task. If the little voice inside says, "I don't feel like doing that today," you can respond by saying, "I don't feel like it, but I'm doing it, anyway." Wanting to do something isn't required for doing it. It's helpful to bring to mind why the activity is on your calendar in the first place and how it could benefit you.

Transition planning

Although this is the last of the five phases, it is by no means the last to occur. Like the others, this stage is not finite. You don't enter and complete it. It's an ongoing process.

A transition plan is a blueprint that displays the proposed path of a transition. It's the directions, the Waze of transitioning, if you will. We identify a destination and we choose the route. But sometimes the route changes. It gets longer or shorter, goes off course on back roads, or hits a detour. We can't control the traffic or predict the pace. Once we identify our plan and have the steps in place, it's time to let go of expectations and just go with it. Transitioning out of sport, like traveling along the interstate, is unpredictable, and we are best served by bringing a combination of flexibility, commitment, and openness to experiences we might never have imagined for ourselves.

An effective transition plan is not a backup plan. It's not a plan B or a consolation. It's a plan that has meaning. It's part of our life story. Develop a plan that excites you even though you might not be ready for it while you're still competing. Having a plan creates a more versatile, well-rounded version of yourself. Preparing to transition out of sport is a mental, emotional, and physical journey. It's about transitioning into life.

***

I had no transition plan to exit cycling. My transition began with physical nudges—tight IT bands, and back pain. I muscled through as my body failed me, and my desire to spend hours a week on my bike diminished. I couldn't admit to myself, let alone anyone else, that cycling and I were parting ways.

I remember the phone rang one weekend morning at a time I would typically have been out riding. I didn't answer. I listened to the message play. "Hi, Beth. Call me when you're back from your ride."

I was sitting on my couch.

In my pajamas.

Cringing.

This pattern went on for a little while. As my time on the bike lessened, I faced new questions and doubts about myself. Who was I without cycling? I had not yet entered the acceptance phase I described earlier.

Part of my struggle with this transition was that I thought I needed to remove cycling from my story to move forward. But what I really needed was to integrate my cycling experiences into my story and press on with a new narrative. That narrative would capture the joy, beauty, failures, and struggles of cycling, and, most of all, my will to push new limits, try new things, and be true to myself.

I appreciate that if I, an average athlete, had a difficult transition, more accomplished athletes are facing more critical challenges. It's helpful to bring the same attributes that led to success in sport to the transition out of it and into the next stages of life. To that point, there's an old saying that an athlete dies twice. The first "death" is when they leave their sport. But

I see it differently. When an athlete transitions practically and proactively, they don't die twice, they live twice.

References

[1] World Health Organization. (n.d.). Promoting mental health. Retrieved September 7, 2022, from https://www.who.int/westernpacific/activities/promoting-mental-health

[2] Brewer, B. W., & Petitpas, A. J. (2017). Athletic identity foreclosure. Current Opinion in Psychology, 16, 118–122. https://doi.org/10.1016/j.copsyc.2017.05.004.

[3] David Lavallee (2019) Engagement in Sport Career Transition Planning Enhances Performance, Journal of Loss and Trauma, 24:1, 1–8, DOI: 10.1080/15325024.2018.1516916.

ABOUT BETH

Beth Lorell provides therapy to individuals and teaches mental health awareness and communication strategies. Her background is in clinical social work and public health. For over twenty years, she has helped individuals overcome the effects of anxiety, depression, and trauma so they can live their best lives. Beth has worked on the front lines and in leadership positions in both suburban and inner-city communities.

As an athlete herself, Beth understands the connection between mental health and performance. She helps athletes achieve positive mental health and teaches coaches to support athletes' mental health while they pursue performance excellence. Beth works under the premise that an organization can champion mental health and promote a culture of well-being while running a thriving, elite sport program.

CHAPTER 10

THE MINIMUM STANDARD

BY STEVE MELLOR

Christmas has always been a special day for me, filled with joy, laughter, and cherished memories. It's a day to be with those you love, sing carols, exchange gifts, and indulge in delicious food. But on Christmas Day of 2010, everything felt different. The holiday that I had always looked forward to with eager anticipation had lost its luster, and my heart was heavy with a sense of loss and disappointment. There were no gifts to unwrap, no hilarious stories to share, no embarrassing sweaters to wear, and no amount of food that could bring me into a good headspace.

As I reflected on where I was in life on this day of good cheer, I was doing everything in my power to avoid attention. Why would someone want to celebrate me? Spending Christmas in the U.S. with a close friend and their family has become a common occurrence for me over the past six years.

My family in England and I probably found a financial argument to qualify my staying on U.S. soil, but I appreciated being able to avoid the possibility of having to be my usual self with my family. They didn't know at the time, but that guy was disappearing before my eyes.

Almost two years on from when I swam my last race, I could recognize that I was living life on a moving walkway, standing still while I drifted along without purpose, without direction, and without intent.

No matter where I would show up, I felt like a churned-up and spit-out version of my old self who no longer cared about how he treated himself and others. Where did it all go wrong?

Two years ago, despite sustaining an injury that hampered my final season of swimming, I had objectives. I trained with the required discipline even while physically limited. I brought energy to those around me, so they remained focused on optimal performance.

I prided myself on bringing the best version of myself to the pool and to all areas of life every day. I was the voice others needed, the example others aspired to, and the standard for professionalism.

At that point in life, simply put, I was the only version of myself I had ever known. But little did I know then that I was saying goodbye to a version of myself I would never see again.

Leaving your athletic career behind can seem like going from an answer book to a book of questions. As an athlete, I had all the answers, or at least knew where to get them. Feedback was constant throughout training. Whether it be the stopwatch, the data, or the ability to get your hand on the wall first, you knew where you stood.

Competition delivered results, the simplest answers in the world! Win or lose, lifetime best performance or not, the answer revealed itself, and you knew where you stood.

The daily grind of my life as a competitive swimmer was a routine so ingrained in my psyche that I could almost do it in my sleep. Wake up, practice, eat, sleep, study, repeat - it was a never-ending cycle that I had committed to with all my heart. There were times when it felt like my body had a voice of its own, and it would tell me what I needed to do next, when it needed to be done, and what came next in the day.

Then came the day that voice I trusted and relied upon started to speak less and less and eventually went silent on me. It no longer knew what it should be doing, suddenly allowing life and the routine of others to dictate where I would go and what I would do. So where did that voice go? Furthermore, where did it originate in the first place? It had to be created at some point. What was it born from? How did it know why and when it needed to speak up? Did it not realize the integral role it was playing in creating purpose and providing answers? To say that I had taken that voice and that level of intent for granted throughout my athletic career was an understatement.

As I searched for clues and answers to these questions over the course of those first two years after retiring from swimming, the one shred of sense of self I had been able to hold onto was the competitor within me. He was not gone. He existed, albeit in a disoriented state, and he was adamant about reestablishing the standards that once made up the competitive swimmer that I was.

The more I explored this competitor, the more I recognized that those standards I implemented were rock solid; they were unbreakable! I refused nothing beneath such standards from either myself or those around me.

I can recall how I prided myself on delivering a daily output that would represent what I qualified as a successful day. It was the bare minimum I expected from myself while also being a standard few others could keep up with. A Minimum Standard, if you will … it took me almost two years, but something about the term "minimum standard" resonated with me. I had to explore that further.

What are minimum standards?

As athletes, we all face minimum standards at some point in our sporting journey. These standards may not always be obvious, but they are often disguised within the rules and expectations of our respective sports. For example, we may need to master a particular skill or routine in order to remain competitive, or we may have specific requirements for our age group that we must meet to stay in the game. And if we aspire to achieve elite performance, we may need to tap into our innermost desires and keep pushing through times of adversity.

Now, I understand if you're a bit confused at this point. When you hear the term "minimum standards," you may think of the bare minimum required to meet certain criteria, such as the consideration standards for making a school team, or the attendance requirements for staying on a team. But I want to turn this negative term on its head. As competitive athletes, we hold ourselves to higher and non-negotiable standards that we expect not only from ourselves but from those around us and our environment. This is what sets us apart from the rest. We don't just settle for meeting the bare minimum; we strive for excellence in everything we do.

Throughout my swimming career, I refused to be outworked, insisted on carrying myself as a professional, and strived to lead and motivate others to reach their potential. I had standards for my everyday approach to my sport that were unwavering, even during the most adverse times of disappointment and injury. This fabric of my DNA and make-up for who I was as a swimmer were my minimum standards to have even a chance of success!

Like many athletes, however, my story was one of transition, finding a way to navigate the real world and interpret what my minimum standards now needed to be. I was interpreting standards as being drastically lower than what I had held myself to for so long, naturally losing myself through this process.

So, the notion I presented myself with was how to reestablish the minimum standards that made me the athlete I once was in these unfamiliar and non-athletic surroundings.

While the situation I found myself in seemed bleak, by simply identifying and labeling a term like "minimum standards," I felt I had taken back some control of where I found myself. I couldn't help but wonder what had happened to the athlete I used to be. I missed the days when I was a training partner and an inspiration to those around me. I had always tried to lead by example, setting the bar high and demonstrating why it was important to instill a minimum standard in everything we do. It was a key part of what gave me a competitive edge and made me the athlete I was.

But now, as I searched for that same fire and drive within me,

I realized that I could be my own source of inspiration. If I could live out my own values and beliefs, and be the best version of myself, I could once again become the example to others of why it's important to strive for excellence. This could be my chance to reconnect with the competitor within me and rediscover what made me strive for greatness. Furthermore, if implemented effectively, it felt like it could become my superpower!

But before I get too far ahead, I want to ensure you have been able to completely understand where I am coming from with the term, "minimum standards." For instance, how do you know if you have minimum standards? I have personally defined my minimum standard as the performance or effort I expect of myself in order to be able to accept an outcome. To be clear, this is not my way of saying, "Every time I go out there, I give it my all."

You will have learned through sports how that just isn't realistic and is too much to expect of yourself. It is an exhaustive approach to performance and execution that can create problems and leave a person feeling like they are constantly failing.

A minimum standard is something you take pride in, something that, on your worse day, guarantees you will still accomplish something. It demonstrates to those around you that you live with an expectation of yourself.

Something else you might be thinking here is how I simply had "high expectations" for myself as an athlete and am just labeling this age-old term differently. I don't think so.

If this was about having high expectations for yourself and those around you, you would not be addressing essential standards, the ones that ensure progress and impact even on the most difficult of days. A high expectation is also something a person can avoid taking ownership of, as it is typically more of a theoretical or potential standard to aspire to, but not necessarily an expectation.

In short, your minimum standards should define you at your best and at your worst, down to your core.

To go back to me as an athlete for a moment, I rarely stopped and acknowledged these foundations of what made me the athlete I was. An athlete acknowledging why they are successful? Are you crazy? That requires putting the spotlight on yourself in a world where you are taught to knuckle down and get on with things.

If I slowed down or got distracted, I would hear my coaches say something along the lines of, "We don't have time to stop," or "Pull your head out the clouds, Mellor, and focus on what we are doing."

Yet, if we actually stop and acknowledge what makes us who we are, we might notice how our minimum standards as athletes were there all along:

- What were your habits or the expectations you had of yourself?
- What would cause you to feel guilty or as if you had lost ground somehow?
- What moments provided a sense of accomplishment or satisfaction?

As you dive into this train of thought, you are reminded of the practices and drills you crushed. Maybe you recount moments in a competition where you made a mistake that cost you. Maybe you also consider times in training when you took steps to make amendments for prior errors.

The common factor in all these moments is that, whether in success or failure, you were learning to establish minimum standards you would hold yourself to in order to complete the task at hand.

The fact was that as an athlete, my minimum standards were high, which I don't share for some egotistical reason. I was an athlete that knew I had limits when it came to pure natural talent. Fortunately, I recognized and embraced this early enough to establish and incorporate minimum standards that would counteract my limitations.

My day-to-day mindset had to make up for the talent I lacked as I utilized an ambition that burned strongly enough not to waste the opportunity at hand.

But on that Christmas day, almost two years after my athletic retirement, I was starting to realize I didn't know how *not* to be an athlete. And in that realization, I was looking to connect the present moment with a time in life when I felt I recognized who I was. By doing this, I came to the realization that I once had these lofty minimum standards that allowed me to flourish in what felt like a past life as an athlete. While that was a great realization to have, the next step was knowing what to do with it.

Pulling from our past

It was apparent that based on two years of living without purpose, upon athletic retirement, I felt I needed to leave the past behind and simply get on with life now. This was clearly not the best thing to serve me and my future, but I can't help but think I was not the first and won't be the last athlete to do so. The important thing was that I was finally connecting the dots between the present and the past in how my past could, in fact, teach me how best to live in the present.

By recognizing I had lost my minimum standards, I was pulling from my past as opposed to avoiding it, grabbing my past by the horns and dragging it into the present day, where I desperately needed it.

In doing so, I was bringing the person I had already built within me back to the surface after two years of pushing him away. My past taught me that to be a successful swimmer, I had to establish minimum standards for training, nutrition, recovery, performance, and relationships with teammates. Now I needed to establish the minimum standards required for the life I felt I was capable of living.

I looked at how I could do this with my daily workload:

⇒   How often do I need to work?
⇒   How much work will be enough work?
⇒   How will I measure the effectiveness of my efforts?

I analyzed the minimum expectations I was looking for in the relationships I had in my life:

I need relationships that…

⇒   Allow me to be my authentic self
⇒   Motivate me to work
⇒   Push me to want to be a good friend

I knew I had to prioritize how I would exercise and treat my body:

⇒ In what ways do I plan to exercise, and to what intensity?
⇒ Is there a performance element I still want to satisfy?
⇒ What standard will I strive toward achieving?

And as I focused on establishing these standards within my life, I began to inundate myself with insight into who I was and wanted to be. I discovered I wanted to work—like really work hard—and apply myself towards passions and projects where I could compete against myself and demand I pursue what I am capable of.

I wanted to pay better attention to what my body was telling me throughout and at the end of the day so as to build feedback on how well I was applying myself and following my intentions. I knew I needed to reinvest in others, and I also needed them to demand and expect more of me. I was forming accountability. I was closing in on my old self. I could sense minimum standards forming.

What I thought would be a fairly simple exercise became an incredible adjustment. After almost two years of feeling bad at the end of the day and waking up most days feeling even worse, I suddenly had some measurables. At day's end, I had indications that I could assess throughout my day in the areas I had potentially fallen short on a recently established minimum standard.

I found growth opportunities in ending the day in a self-reflective state and asking:

⇒ Why do I feel bad tonight?
⇒ What is the reason for feeling a little lost this evening?
⇒ What can I learn from today?

I rediscovered my ability to reflect, coach, and analyze from within, and look to the next day as an opportunity to make amends for any standard I slipped below.

Possibly the greatest impact, however, that came from looking at my past was being rattled by the very obvious absence of what I had always defined as success. For you, it might be scoring goals, claiming victories, hitting personal bests, mastering new routines, etc., but for me, it was the ability to accurately assess my efforts with time.

The watch never lied in the pool, and it made my time swimming black and white; it was either fast enough, or it was not. I found in minimum standards a reassurance that I could assess progression, even without the immediate feedback I once received in sports.

Even though there will always be opportunities to go and claim victories, the truth was that progress was now the greatest indicator of success. If I can't wait around all day hoping to see a win, I can certainly work towards it.

If I can no longer see an obvious chance to claim a victory, I can look to win in educating myself for future growth. If I felt I could not compete in a certain area, I could challenge myself to get out of my comfort zone in another way and seek that sense of competition.

Allow minimum standards to bring out your competitive self

Are you separating yourself from those around you? Are you incentivizing yourself to step up your efforts? Have you invested yourself in the performance and outcome of others? The day you are able to answer yes to all of these questions is the day you know minimum standards have become an integral part of your DNA once more.

Shift expectations to being more resourceful, where you embrace expectations, habits, decisions, and self-awareness. We are born and bred competitors that are wrestling with the notion of losing our competitive edge. Your minimum standards will allow you to accept who you are and the path you have chosen.

After all, minimum standards are what sparked our competitive nature in the first place. "I won't let my brother beat me," "I know I'm better than that," "she may be bigger than me, I just know I have to outwork her."

We insisted that there were standards we were too good to drop below in these moments. So, today, what standards are you refusing to drop below?

The concept of minimum standard in athletics goes beyond just setting your sights on the ultimate goal. It's about embracing the person you see in the mirror each day and trusting that you are doing everything in your power to achieve your goals, even when the outcome is not what you hoped for.

As an athlete, you learn to cope with defeat and move on from the losses that once felt insurmountable. But for some, the end of an athletic career can feel like the biggest defeat of all, and it can be hard to find the strength to move forward. If you find yourself in this position, know that there is still a path forward.

By adopting a mindset of minimum standards, and embracing the best version of yourself each day, you can learn to redefine your goals and find new sources of motivation and fulfillment in life beyond athletics.

Incorporate your minimum standards again, and you will rediscover and establish the person who made your athletic career possible. You will have your north star, the shining light that will guide you when answers seem unavailable.

So, start today. If setting goals seems too difficult, then set habits instead. If you no longer trust yourself, reestablish instincts within yourself that you trust. Furthermore, go and build confidence by not hiding from life and injecting yourself into areas of uncertainty, knowing you can lean on minimum standards when necessary.

A decade on from that dark Christmas, I can say I have a lot more answers than questions about how I go about life. But if you start asking the right difficult questions, you will soon take solace in the fact that you had the answers inside of you all along.

So, tell me…what are your Minimum Standards?

ABOUT STEVE

Steve Mellor is a former top-50 world-ranked swimmer for Great Britain and a former Olympic-level Swim Coach. Today, he is a business owner, executive coach, author, and keynote speaker under his company Career Competitor. A native of England, Steve spent most of the 2000s in the United States as a collegiate swimmer and swim coach. He competed in college at North Carolina State, where he was a three-time school record holder, NCAA Championships qualifier, and three-time ACC Championships silver medalist.

Following his time at NC State, where he graduated with a Bachelor of Arts in Communications and a Master of Science in Management, Steve spent most of the next decade working towards becoming the Associate Head Coach with Louisiana State University. At LSU, Steve guided athletes to NCAA and SEC Swimming heights, and he was behind LSU's first-ever American Olympic swimmer, Brooks Curry, who went on to win an Olympic Gold Medal with Team USA.

In October 2021, Steve turned his passion for optimizing individual and team performance into founding his company, Career Competitor LLC, where he serves as an executive coach, a culture consultant, and a keynote speaker. The company grew from the Career Competitor podcast that began in June 2018 and still runs today, where former athletes and established competitors discuss how they optimize their competitive and athlete-minded characteristics to reach great heights in their careers.

The following year, Steve also became an author with his book, *SHOCK THE WORLD! A Competitor's Guide to Realizing Your Potential.*

Last but certainly not least, he is the proud husband of Britney and father to his children, Eleanor and Jacob.

CHAPTER 11

THE POWER OF LOVE & RESILIENCE: AN ATHLETE'S JOURNEY

BY ERIKA FAY

'm sitting on my couch with a cup of tea and a magazine, ready to decompress after a long day of work. I just finished leading a workshop for a group of student-athletes, pouring out every ounce of energy, and looking forward to celebrating by relaxing, reading, and enjoying my warm tea. Or so I thought.

As I take a sip, my partner's voice suddenly cuts through the peaceful silence, and my heart stops. He tells me that he wants to end our relationship. At that moment, my mind goes blank. I can't process what he's saying. This can't be happening. Not now.

As he continues to speak, the reality of the situation sets in. My heart sinks as I try to wrap my head around what this means for our family and for me.

I have been through my fair share of breakups, and they never get easier. I've been a serial monogamist for most of my life, always enjoying sharing my life with a partner and believing that I really do have a soulmate. But, as much as I hate to admit it, I've had my heart broken more times than I can count. Breakups are always painful, no matter how many times you have gone through them.

Looking back on my past relationships, I know that I played a role in every breakup. Maybe I didn't see it at the time, but I know it is true. Even when I was the one ending things, there was a part of me that felt heartbroken that it was not going to work out.

While sitting on my couch, trying to make sense of everything my partner has just said, I struggle to remind myself that this is simply another chapter in my life.

Since I was a little girl, I've known that I wanted to be a mother and have a family of my own. It was something I dreamed about constantly - the idea of being happily married to my soulmate, the love of my life, and having children together.

As I grew older, that dream only became more pronounced. I started dating in high school, searching for someone who I could see myself building a life with. I fell in love easily, always envisioning a future together. But as each relationship ended, I was left feeling lost and hopeless.

Despite the setbacks, I never gave up on the dream of having a family. I knew that I would find my soulmate someday, and we would create the happy family that I had always envisioned. It was a beacon of hope that kept me going through the rough patches.

Over ten years ago, I sat in front of my computer browsing Facebook when I stumbled upon my friend's new baby photos with her husband. Initially, I felt elated for them as I scrolled through the pictures, but suddenly tears started streaming down my face as sadness consumed me.

At the age of thirty-six, as I was looking at her photos, it really hit me. I felt my lifelong dream of having a baby slipping away. This was not the first of my friends to have a baby—most of my friends were mothers. I was surprised by my reaction.

I recall thinking, "I am so happy for them, but why do I feel so sad?" Have you ever encountered a similar situation where you experienced conflicting emotions simultaneously? It may not necessarily be related to your friend having a child; it could be any experience that elicits mixed feelings.

As I stared at the pictures of her beautiful family in the hospital room, the gap between where I was in my life and where I desperately wanted to be, felt as wide as the ocean. On the one hand, I was genuinely happy for her. She had always wanted to have a baby, so it was great to see her dreams finally come true. I knew she would make an amazing mother and that her child was lucky to have her.

At the same time though, I couldn't help feeling a sense of sadness and longing. I had always wanted to be a mom too, but for various reasons, it just hadn't happened for me yet. Seeing my friend holding her baby and experiencing all the joys of motherhood reinforced just how much I wanted that for myself.

It was hard to reconcile these conflicting feelings-I didn't want to take away from my friend's happiness, but I also couldn't ignore my own feelings of sadness.

As an athlete, I am driven by goals and identify as a (recovering) Type A personality. I was simultaneously training for my second Ironman and managing a new business venture. I have always been accustomed to achieving the goals I set for myself, but for some reason, this particular goal felt more personal and harder to attain. It seemed to constantly evade me. I felt stuck, and as I sat with tears streaming down my face, I knew that having a baby was something I had no idea how to achieve—but my desire for it was stronger than ever.

Have you ever experienced a sense of unease when a goal or aspiration appears to be slipping out of your grasp, despite typically excelling at achieving what you set out to do? Regardless of the nature of the dream, whether sports-related or not, it is disheartening to feel like a certain aspect of life is not falling into place. Nevertheless as athletes, we understand that in the face of setbacks or seemingly insurmountable odds, we must persist and never give up. This embodies the true essence of the athlete's soul.

Of course, no one becomes an athlete with hopes of losing and struggling. In sport, it is natural for us to want to win games and championships. It is innate to want to continue to exceed what we once saw as our best.

As an athlete, my personal goal wasn't necessarily to become "the best" or the "G.O.A.T" (Greatest of All Time) in my sport. Instead, I aimed to push the boundaries of my own abilities. When faced with the challenge of balancing my athletic and career pursuits with my aspiration of starting a family, I discovered a transformational system that I now teach to others. Through rigorous study and application of this proven, dependable, and replicable system, I learned that any ambitious dream or goal, no matter how daunting, can be turned into a tangible reality within the context of one's life.

Despite sensing one of my dreams slipping away, I was

determined not to allow the prevailing circumstances to discourage me, just as we, as athletes, never give up.

No matter what your aspirations are, I would like to impart some potent principles from this transformational system, that possess the ability to revolutionize your journey and hasten your progress toward accomplishing your dreams. By utilizing these principles, you can circumvent the obstacles I encountered and harness the potency of your innermost desires and unfulfilled aspirations to forge a life and a future that genuinely excites and inspires you.

Crafting a vision

The first principle in this system is crafting a vision. What would you love to see in your life? This may sound simple—especially when it comes to being an athlete. Sometimes goals and dreams (or a vision) are used interchangeably, but I would propose that goals and dreams are different.

Goals are tangible and quantifiable milestones on the path to realizing a dream. A dream or vision is inherently elusive, and we may not have a precise understanding of all the necessary steps or methods to manifest it, but we know that we are passionately devoted to it!

As I mentioned, my desire to give birth to a child with the love of my life and have a family together was a dream I had held since I was a little girl. I have been in love with this dream for as long as I can remember. As the years went on and as each long-term love relationship ended, I questioned the viability of my dream, and it seemed clear that I had no idea how to bring my dream into reality.

While it is evident that formulating a vision is crucial to attaining enduring success in any pursuit, it is relatively uncommon when it pertains to constructing a vision for a life that you adore. A vision comprises a captivating and motivating representation of the future that defines where you aspire to be, what you aim to accomplish, the impact you desire to create, and the person you envisage yourself evolving into along the way.

For example, if you're making the transition from being an athlete to becoming a business owner, you may have a clear understanding of your present circumstances, but you might not be certain of all the stages involved in establishing, operating, expanding, and sustaining a thriving business. Framing a well-defined vision for your enterprise constitutes the primary stride in taking action. If you were to own a business that you adore and take immense pride in, what would it precisely entail? Once you discern your current status and ultimate destination, such as being the owner of a highly prosperous and gratifying business, you are more inclined to undertake motivated action that aligns you with this vision.

Below are some useful guidelines for creating a vision that you will adore:

1. **Reflect on your values and purpose:** Before you can craft a compelling vision, you need to have a clear understanding of what you stand for and what you want to achieve. Reflect on your personal and professional values and pur-

pose. Consider the impact you want to have both personally and professionally.

2. **Ask the question, What would I really love?:** To craft a compelling vision, begin by asking yourself the question, "What would I truly love?" This question is the perfect starting point for creating a vision that is aligned with your deepest desires and aspirations. Instead of limiting yourself to what seems probable or possible, allow yourself to dream big and envision what you would love to experience in your relationships, career, health, freedom (both time and money), and other areas of your life. By listening for what emerges as you ask this question and embracing your truest longings and desires, you can create a vision that inspires and motivates you. Remember, not knowing how you will achieve this vision is okay, as the most important part is to lean into your truest desires and allow the vision to guide you toward them.

3. **Envision the future and define your mission:** Once you have a clear understanding of your values, purpose, and what you would love for your life, take some time to envision the future you want to create. Imagine what success looks like and how your life contributes to your family, community, and society. Afterward, define your mission by crafting a statement that encapsulates what you stand for, what you do, who you serve, and why you do it. Your mission statement should embody the core of your values and the impact you wish to create with your life, and it

can serve as a guide for your actions. It should be succinct, clear, and inspiring.

4. **Craft your vision statement:** Your vision statement is a vivid and captivating portrayal of the future that you desire to create. It serves as a source of inspiration and motivation for you. To make your vision statement even more potent, articulate it in the present tense as if it is already happening. For instance, you can start with the phrase, "I am overjoyed and thankful that…" It is essential to be specific, select words that stir your emotions, and illustrate your life as if you have already accomplished everything and are living your ideal life.

After creating your vision statement, it's crucial to be selective about who you share it with. Some of your trusted friends or family members may have doubts about what you can achieve, not because they don't care for you but because they don't want to see you disappointed. I know this from some experiences I have had with friends who deeply care for me. You are always the highest authority on what you would love to bring forth in your life. It's essential to review and refine your vision periodically to ensure it remains something you truly love. Your vision should guide your strategy, action, and decision-making. This leads us to the next principle, the power of decision.

Power of decision

Going back to the couch for a moment–as I listened and my partner ended our relationship, my mind was consumed with confusion and overwhelming emotions. Nevertheless, a small voice reminded me that I had the power to decide what to do next. I could either let this situation crush me or choose to acknowledge that it was not what I wanted, give myself time to grieve, recommit to my vision, allow myself to feel the emotions, and grow through the pain.

After experiencing heartbreak, relationship pain can be unbearable, causing some to completely abandon the idea of finding love again. Unfortunately, many of us respond in ways that impede our chances of having a healthy, loving relationship. Some isolate themselves, while others settle for emotionally unavailable partners due to a desperate desire for love. Fear is often the underlying cause of this behavior, preventing us from fully committing ourselves to a relationship. To overcome this, it is crucial to make decisions based on our vision, rather than fear.

To be clear, I am not implying that the process of grieving is simple or pleasant. On the contrary, it can be arduous, marked by restless nights, uncertainty, dread, loneliness, and pessimistic thoughts. There were instances where I felt inundated by the agony, which persisted for days or even weeks. Nevertheless, I opt to stay committed to my dream and persevere. Even during times when everything appears to be crumbling, I reiterate my devotion to my vision. This is the potency of decision.

Pain is an inevitable part of the human experience, and it can feel overwhelming, especially when it seems never-ending. At times, it may even lead us to question our ability to continue. Unfortunately, too many people have reached a point where the pain becomes too much, and they take their own lives. It can be challenging to imagine a future or commit to a dream when we are in deep emotional turmoil, but it IS possible.

In these moments we can tap into the soul of an athlete, by believing and trusting that although we cannot always see the big picture, it is still there. I believe there is a unique and divine reason for each of our lives, and it is our birthright to live a life that feels fulfilling, connected, and purpose-driven, even when it seems like there is no way out or through. Unfortunately, too many of us have not believed this.

To pursue our dreams in the face of life's greatest challenges and trust that fulfillment is still possible is to exercise the power of decision. This means committing to our vision even in the absence of a clear roadmap or when we feel like it is impossible. It is a resilient move that requires us to make choices that serve our vision.

Although we often desire a clear and comprehensive roadmap to follow toward achieving our dreams, there are times when we may only have a vague idea and no definitive path to take. Nonetheless, we still have the power to make a choice. For me, I have made the decision to allow myself the time to heal and process my emotions before embarking on a new romantic journey. My resolve is firm; I refuse to relinquish my desire for love. Although my original plan may need to be altered, my dream of finding my soulmate and building a family is still unwavering. The fundamental essence of my dream, which is the love and connection between us, remains constant.

The unwavering commitment to our dreams should not only manifest in one area of our lives. To truly live a fulfilling life, one that aligns with our soul, we must embody this resilience and dedication in all aspects of our existence, including career, relationships, health, and personal freedom.

This is the third tenet of the transformation system, which involves practicing living as the person who has already achieved the life we aspire to lead.

Acting as the person living the dream

One place you may have already practiced this principle, is in your sport. I know that each of us may have wildly different relationships with our sport. But you acted as the athlete with your focus on the vision. I would guess most of us can relate to getting ourselves out of bed on a cold (or sweltering hot) morning for practice when we *really* did not feel like it. Your commitment to your outcome (your vision) overrode the feeling.

I can easily re-live my experience as a swimmer, with two-a-day practices and those cold early mornings before the sun was even up, sitting on the pool deck looking at the water and thinking, "I REALLY don't want to jump in."

And in water polo tournaments, after multiple games in a day, sitting on the pool deck with milk in my goggles and my goggles on my face, (to neutralize the sting) because my eyes were burning so badly from the chlorine, I could barely see. Despite the brutal conditions, we never gave up. We may have been exhausted and sore, with milk in our goggles and a burning sensation in our eyes, but we were determined to play the next game. And that is exactly what we did.

It is funny to think back on it now and wonder if people still use milk in their goggles to ease the sting of chlorine. That trick might have been the norm back in the 90s when I played water polo, but I can only imagine how things have changed since then.

Still, no matter how much time has passed, the resilience and perseverance that we learned on the pool deck and in the water are lessons that have stayed with us long after we played our final game.

Resilience

As I continue to commit to my dream, and as you gain greater clarity and commit to yours, resilience is a valuable quality for us to practice. You likely already understand its importance. It helps us overcome setbacks and challenges, whether they occur in sports, careers, relationships, health, or any other area of life. With resilience, we can bounce back and continue to pursue our goals and vision.

In addition, resilience and the power of decision are closely linked. This includes the ability to stay focused and motivated even in the face of adversity. Through practicing decision-making and building resilience, we can perform better under pressure and stay committed to our goals no matter the circumstances, not just in sports but in all aspects of life.

To continue to increase your resilience, here are some actions you can take:

Practice positive self-talk: During challenging times, it can be easy to fall into negative thinking patterns. However, by practicing positive self-talk, you can train yourself to focus on the things you can control and maintain a growth mind-set. For example, instead of thinking, "I can't do this," try thinking, "I'm giving it my best shot."

Be open-minded: To cultivate resilience, it's important to be coachable and open-minded. This means being willing to try new things and stepping out of your comfort zone to experiment with new techniques or strategies that can help you improve. Being open-minded also means being receptive to innovative ideas and perspectives, even if they challenge your current beliefs or practices. By embracing new opportunities for growth and learning, you can develop the resilience necessary to overcome setbacks and achieve your goals.

Take responsibility: Resilience also means taking responsibility for your actions and owning up to your mistakes. It can be difficult to do this, but it is the ultimate act of resilience. Be accountable for your actions and reactions and be willing to learn from your failures as well as your successes.

Ever since that night on the couch, I have been diligently practicing all three of these resilience practices. Have I been flawless in my execution? Not even close. But I have come to realize that just like physical training, resilience practices take time, repetition, and effort to develop and improve. It is important to remind ourselves that we have the power to grow and develop our skills with practice and dedication. Stay open to new experiences, and you will improve your resilience not only as an athlete but also in all areas of life. This leads me to my final tenet in the transformational system, and that is to get support.

Get Support: Take a moment to reflect on what motivates you to keep improving and stay committed to your goals. When we combine our vision with support, we become unstoppable.

A great coach can recognize potential in us that we may not even see in ourselves. They can help us connect with our true potential and guide us toward achieving our goals and dreams. My best coaches inspired me to compete, to push beyond my perceived limits, and to set my sights high.

Perhaps you've had a coach who did the same for you. It's important to remember that even the best coaching will not make a difference if you are not open to being coached.

Being coachable requires resilience, clear goals, and a strong vision. Without a vision, there's little motivation to persevere as the person who is living the life they desire. Throughout my life, my coach and mentors have provided essential support during challenging periods of transition and other obstacles.

Asking for support is a highly resilient move. It shows that although you may already be strong, you are even stronger with someone supporting you. It is a recognition that sometimes we need someone from the outside to see more in us than we can see in ourselves.

Vision, the power of decision, and resilience come from tapping into the soul of the athlete within us. It resides within each of us and allows us to persist even when we are exhausted, heartbroken, and ready to give up. Our passion for our vision is what motivates us to persevere.

Reap the results

It's funny how the fruits of our labor often reveal themselves in the most unexpected ways. We may have spent countless hours, days, and weeks working towards something, yet it seems as if progress is slow or nonexistent.

However, the fruits of our commitment, decision, and hard work can manifest in miraculous ways when we least anticipate them. Perhaps, as an athlete, you've had periods where you felt like you've hit a plateau in your training or competition, but out of nowhere, you received a valuable opportunity or unexpected support that reignited your passion and motivation to continue striving for excellence. Or maybe you've been toiling away at a personal project for months, and just when you were about to throw in the towel, you receive recognition or support from an unexpected source.

Through my unwavering commitment to my vision and the practice of these principles, I visualized myself as the woman who was already living my dream. And, in ways beyond my imagination, the universe rewarded me. Despite it seeming impossible, I became a mother.

The key is to trust the process, maintain focus, and be open to receiving the rewards that come our way. By working with the principles I have shared with you, my life was transformed, even without knowing how it would all work out. I embodied the person I had envisioned for myself, and after nearly a decade, my partner and I were blessed with a natural pregnancy when I was forty-five. The following year, I gave birth to a healthy baby boy named Liam. This August, we will celebrate my son's fourth birthday, fulfilling my once-distant vision.

My intention for this chapter is to encourage and inspire greater levels of gratitude and commitment to your life and your dreams. I also encourage you to practice the principles I have shared here as you journey toward fulfilling your dreams.

As athletes, we are familiar with setbacks, such as the physical and emotional pain of injuries and the inevitability of our sports careers ending or changing. Like my dream, sometimes the details look a little different than we thought. When it is clear we are being redirected, we continue to move forward, being guided by the question "What would I love?" I am going through a similar process now, as the partnership with my son's father ended about a year ago.

We can use challenges and setbacks to evaluate our commitment to our vision. When one door closes, we can choose to abandon or endure, but we should never give up out of fear, frustration, or anger. Sometimes challenges and setbacks are qualifiers to prepare us for something even greater. Instead of being discouraged, we can use the question "What would I love?" to guide our decisions and actions, taking steps to serve our vision. In my case, my evolved vision includes fostering a relationship of respect and love with my son's father as co-parents, ultimately finding love again, and welcoming a bonus father figure into my son's life.

Pursuing our dreams requires both resilience and vulnerability, but the rewards are well worth it. By committing to our vision and embodying the belief that we are already living it, certain aspects of our current life may begin to fall away. It is important to remember this is not a sign of things falling apart but rather falling into place. And to keep in mind that the principles of this system can work for anyone. Each one of us has the power to create the life we truly desire.

As you journey through life, always remember that you possess immense power. Even in moments of doubt, I encourage you to tap into the same inner strength that carried you through physical exhaustion and pushed you to keep going. You are capable of greatness and possess incredible strength, love, and resilience beyond what you may realize.

As I write this chapter, I do not know how my dream will all come together, but I assure you, I will continue to utilize the very strategies I have shared with you. And instead of being riddled with anxiety, I am filled with a sense of calm assurance that whatever lies ahead will be nothing short of amazing. I surrender to the mastery of these principles, being guided by love, riding the waves of the unpredictability of life, and I trust that everything will work out exquisitely.

ABOUT ERIKA

Erika Fay is the highly accomplished and sought-after President of Maximum Achievement Coaching, dedicated to empowering athletes to achieve their peak performance both on and off the field. With over 20 years of experience as a Psychotherapist, Best Selling Author, and Award-winning Success Coach, Erika has transformed the lives and careers of countless professional and amateur athletes, as well as entrepreneurs, from all around the world.

Erika is renowned for her dynamic approach that combines inspiring workshops and in-depth coaching programs, which turn clients' ideas into life-changing actions. Her exceptional ability to unlock her clients' potential and help them achieve new heights of success sets her apart as a true leader in the field of coaching.

Erika has been featured on several high-profile platforms, including Good Day Chicago, The Best Coaches Series on Best You TV, The Brian & Justin Show, and many more. As a former athlete at Purdue University, Erika continues to pursue her passion for athletics, having completed two full Ironman distance triathlons, 36 marathons, and multiple marathons and triathlons per year.

Whether you are an elite athlete looking to maximize your potential or an entrepreneur seeking to reach new heights of success, Erika's unparalleled expertise and exceptional coaching style are guaranteed to help you achieve your goals.

Connect with Erika at www.maximumachievement coaching.com or on Instagram @erikafay.

CHAPTER 12

REDEFINING SUCCESS AFTER ATHLETICS

BY KELSEY WIECHMAN

This is my story from growing up as an athlete, playing as a collegiate ice hockey goalie, to the present, where I'm in a successful 15+-year career in corporate America. I'll share my personal reflections about my athletic career and my transition out of sports, which have only been made clear after having enough distance to see the impact. As I've reflected on my journey, the most impactful insight I've gained is how difficult it has been to define my identity and my success after the veil of athletics was lifted. I'll conclude by sharing guidance for anyone experiencing a similar transition.

Youth sports

Imagine a typical summer day, where the temperature fluctuates from a comfortable 70 degrees in the morning as the bright sun rises to kick start your day. The temperature drops to a chilly 50 degrees in the afternoon, and then spikes to a sweltering 90 degrees by early evening as that same sun beats down on you with unrelenting heat. That's common, right? No? Is that not what everyone else experiences?

Well, that was my typical summer growing up. I started my mornings in Minnesota at an outdoor swimming pool for swim practice, then went to an ice arena for a few hours for hockey practice, and finished out the day at the soccer field for a game. That was my summer routine as a kid playing multiple sports. Cool. Frigid. Hot. Eat. Sleep. Repeat.

Growing up, I participated in a variety of sports. Although I dedicated most of my time and energy as a kid to soccer and hockey, I also tried gymnastics, dance, tennis, cheerleading, figure skating, and T-ball.

High school sports

My high school years were formative. Beyond education, I was developing skills, my personality, friendships, and my identity. By high school, my primary sports became hockey, soccer, and golf.

At the time, success was easily defined, especially as an athlete. You either made the team or were cut from the team. We either won the game or lost the game. The puck either goes in the net to score a goal, or the goalie saves it to prevent the goal. The golf ball either flies straight down the fairway, or you shank it left and it gets lost in the trees. Metrics, success, and goals were easy to understand and to strive for.

College: Ice hockey goalie

I went to a Division III college and played hockey. Being a hockey goalie was my primary identity. During a time in my life when I was trying to understand who I was, being a hockey goalie was what made me feel special. I wouldn't have admitted it at the time, but I can now see how much I enjoyed the look of surprise when I introduced myself as a collegiate hockey goalie. And I can also now admit that I loved the external validation that came with being an athlete.

I liked surprising people—and impressing them. I know how shallow that sounds, but that was my reality. The compliments and accolades fueled my drive and motivation to succeed. Ultimately, being successful was what defined me, and my success was measured by achievements and other people's opinions.

While playing, I'd strive to be the very best. During every game, I was determined to be the standout on the ice. Giving my all was all I knew. It never occurred to me—or I didn't have it in me—to only give partial effort. I feared not being an exceptional athlete.

The real world: professional career

When I graduated from college, I had a job lined up at a major retailer, and my last hockey game was only a few months in my rearview mirror. I continued marching forward because that was the only path I knew how to take.

From the outside, it may have seemed like I had it made. In hindsight, I can see clearly how no longer being an athlete impacted my actions and my mental health. That void in my identity meant I no longer felt "exceptional." In response, I shifted my identity.

My foundation was still firmly planted in being a high achiever, but now I needed to be an exceptional employee. The energy I had previously put toward being an athlete I put toward being an employee, and I leaned into the characteristics that had previously made me a successful athlete:

- Driven
- Disciplined
- High-performing
- Self-motivated
- Accountable
- Resilient
- Analytical
- Results-oriented
- Collaborative
- Perfectionistic

Fortunately, those characteristics translated well to being successful in business. Unfortunately, I was still trying to find validation to prove I was an exceptional employee — to myself and to others.

In my pursuit to be an "exceptional employee," I also needed to define what success is in the corporate world. In a challenging job with conflicting priorities and demands, I was left floundering to find clear measures to validate my success.

On a daily basis, with various business crises and changing priorities, success felt impossible to define, much less achieve. But I didn't see any option other than to figure it out.

I again relied on approaches I had used as an athlete to achieve success. I attempted to do it all to find out what would be successful. When things got hard, instead of wisely re-evaluating and adjust my approach, I doubled down on what had previously worked to push me to be the best. I was determined to be the hardest-working, most accountable, best problem-solver, and overall nice, fun team player.

While working in a job that was operating twenty-four hours a day, seven days a week, this was a recipe for disaster—also known as burnout.

I would love to tell you I realized what was happening at that time in my life and made immediate corrections. I wish I could tell you I stopped looking for external praise and instead looked for pride within myself. That's just not true.

It took many years of reflection on those early months of my professional career, and even many hard moments and seasons since, to slowly refine my identity and my version of success. I've come to understand that my identity doesn't have to be solely defined by external factors or traditional definitions of success.

While those aspects may play a role, it can be more expansive, creative and, most importantly, personalized. I've realized that I am the only one who can truly define what success means for my life. I've found a sense of freedom and empowerment to create my own definition of success and live up to the best version I can imagine for myself.

This doesn't mean that I've stopped setting goals or working hard to achieve them. In fact, it's the opposite. Because I've shifted my focus away from what society deems as "successful" to what aligns with my own values and passions, I'm more determined than ever to achieve my personalized version of "success." I have a clear vision for my path ahead toward a fulfilling life that is uniquely my own, and I am more excited than ever to sprint forward.

Navigating transitions

When I transitioned out of athletics, I attempted to recreate the formula for success using the tools and skills I had learned as an athlete.

Although those factors served me well, the problem was that the environment was entirely different. There were different players, rules, and motivations at play. It was like trying to ice skate in a swimming pool. Instead of skates, I should have put on flippers. I needed to see beyond my current situation to reevaluate my entire identity.

I wish I had allowed myself an opportunity to acknowledge the massive transition I was going through, then reconsider the identity I wanted for myself, and lastly, redefine my version of success. Here are my suggestions for navigating transitions:

1. Acknowledge the transition.

   - State the obvious. Get real with yourself about what changed. Consider the ripple impact of the change. Sometimes the changes that hit us the hardest aren't the obvious ones we see coming but the ones that catch us by surprise as secondary waves.

   - Check in on yourself. How is your mental health? What is the story you keep telling yourself? How is your physical health? Don't judge yourself for your answer. Getting clear on where you are starting from is a critical part of the process.

- Connect with others. Talking it out loud can be beneficial in many ways. Not only does this open you up to receive support from others, but by verbalizing what is going on, you are normalizing the situation. Be aware that not everyone will have an ideal response. Some might give you poor advice, and worse yet, some might say hurtful things. This is even more reason to talk to more and more people. You'll receive a lot of advice. The advice that resonates deeply with you is worth the most reflection and consideration.

2. Redefine your identity.
   - Start by doing some deep self-reflection. Take five minutes of quietness — and no, you can't also be scrolling social media for this to work. Ask yourself the following: Who are you? Is this who you want to be? How are past experiences defining you in the present? Do you want them to continue to define you, or let them go? What are your most deeply held values? What are three things you are proud of? Get specific about what is important to you in this moment of your life and why.
   - Then, ask questions of the people closest to you. I know this can feel uncomfortable, but the information you'll get will be invaluable. Ask a few people how they see you. What do they see as your most valuable qualities? How do they see you adding value in your community? I've done this a handful of times in my life, and I continue to think

back to the qualities those trusted people shared with me even years later, and those traits remain a source of pride.

3. Redefine success.
   - Write your goals down. Get clear about what your personal goals are, in addition to your professional goals. Through brainstorming and self-reflection, I created personal goals around physical and mental health, parenting, relationships, and my impact on the community.

For me, I need specific, measurable, and achievable goals to feel accomplished. Make sure you are designing goals that are meaningful to *you*, not anyone else. I often reflect on — and write down — a handful of goals, some of which can be accomplished in the short term (a month or so) and some in the long term (a year or more). This combination is what propels me to make meaningful movement forward — and in the ideal direction.

   - Identify old habits and adjust quickly. You'll never move forward while still being stuck in the same behavior loop. I've become very self-aware when I feel the temptation to fall into old habits. For example, becoming all-consumed by work and neglecting personal responsibilities, or avoiding difficult tasks because I'm overwhelmed by the sheer amount and effort required. When I've felt the temptation of old habits, I've leaned into the discomfort and made time to reflect on what is causing my behavior. The trigger is often the desire to avoid something or someone. Identifying the problem and adjusting has been key to breaking negative patterns and moving forward.

- Accept personal praise. I realized that hearing praise and absorbing praise are different. I had been so accustomed to booming applause and post-game congratulations that the subtle compliments from coworkers and friends could easily go unnoticed. I'm working to acknowledge it and absorb it in order to let myself feel that praise. Those compliments reinforce my progress and further propel me towards success.

I now define success much differently than I did years ago when I was an athlete and differently than when I was a young corporate employee. I'm no longer compelled to be considered "exceptional" and I've learned how to recognize and celebrate even small moments of success. Some examples of my recent goals are running a 5k, teaching my kids to ice skate, organizing a neighborhood cleanup day, and keeping my plants alive.

This is an important moment to pause and explain that this is not an outright "cure" to solve a one-time problem, but rather it's an ongoing practice to continue to reference and refine.

The truth is that I am far from an expert in this space. I still need this practice to ground myself often. In fact, today, while writing this, I've been overwhelmed with the number of things I feel like I need to do: stay committed to a fitness program I signed up for, wrap up requirements for my coaching certification program, finish drafting this chapter, fulfill the demands of my full-time corporate job, and manage the lengthy to-do list for my household.

My instinct is to block out all distractions, get hyper-focused and sprint forward in every direction in order to do it all and at all costs (read: my mental and physical health). The connection between success and achievement, along with external validation, runs deep within me.

Instead, I recognized that the feelings of overwhelm and discomfort are actually an opportunity to focus on myself. I sat in uncomfortable stillness to reflect on figuring out the real priority. What is really necessary in this moment to move forward? How am I aligning myself with my path towards a more fulfilling life? I got clear on my goal for the day, then dedicated my energy toward that pursuit. And here I sit, writing the rest of this chapter as proof.

I'm sharing this with you because we will all go through moments in our lives that push us and change us. Even beyond obvious changes, like a professional change, a relationship change, or ending an athletic career, you are constantly defining and redefining your identity.

This message applies especially to this moment in history when we have gone through a global pandemic. It has changed all of us. It has pushed us all in new and hard ways. I encourage you to take these tools and apply them during this season of your life.

Even if you only take one action from this topic, I encourage you to do this: Take fifteen minutes right now for self-reflection. Acknowledge a recent transition, consider the foundation of your identity, and figure out how you can define success for yourself. Do it. Set a timer right now.

Your newly defined identity and measures of success could be the change you need to reset your outlook on life. Just fifteen minutes can be the catalyst to living a more successful life.

ABOUT KELSEY

Kelsey grew up in the suburbs of Minneapolis, Minnesota. She played various sports growing up and eventually whittled down her primary sport to being an ice hockey goalie. She played Division III hockey for a small, private school in central Minnesota.

Since graduating college, she has been in a successful 15+-year career with a Fortune 50 retailer — with all the expected ups and downs of navigating corporate jobs.

In 2022, Kelsey became a certificated life coach and started After The Jersey Coaching. Her focus is supporting athletes with their transition out of sports. Her approach guides clients to unlock insights and revelations within themselves without being swayed by outside influences. Visit her website at AfterTheJerseyCoaching.com and follow her on Instagram at @AfterTheJerseyCoaching.

Kelsey lives with her husband and daughters in the Twin Cities metro area. They live an active life, balancing work, school, sports, and activities, plus entrepreneurship.

Website: www.AfterTheJerseyCoaching.com

Instagram: @AfterTheJerseyCoaching

LinkedIn: www.linkedin.com/company/after-the-jersey-coaching

Email: AfterTheJersey@gmail.com

CHAPTER 14

ATHLETE RETIREE IDENTITY CONFUSION

BY BRIAN WOOD

Just so we're clear, I was not a big-time athlete. I'm extremely grateful for the basketball memories and experiences at William Paterson University and the traveling teams, pro-am games, and money tournaments around the world after college. But I could not convert my passion for basketball into a bag of cash.

However, even at my modest level as an athlete, I can tell you that transitioning away from the game is tough. You experience identity confusion while also questioning your worth. You feel like you are alone and need to figure out the "now what" portion of life without resources but with an abundance of judgment. You feel like you are the only person on the planet who thinks a certain way.

How does this relate to your next chapter, and how does this connect to leadership, influence, success, pursuing your passion, and leveraging your gifts?

Let's explore.

I'm not crazy (or am I?)

> "Crazy like a fox."
> — Kresley Cole

These are some thoughts an athlete might have:

I've got the ball down low. After initiating about seven head fakes (before the inevitable three-second call) the mindset is:

"If I can just get him to bite, get him up in the air, I can physically beat the shit out of this guy!"

"It would be awesome if the ball were to go in the hoop, but the bigger goal is to drive right through his ribs and hear the sweet sound of him exhaling in agony."

At that point, you can talk all you want but you know I'm stronger than you and that this is going to be a painful night.

Being in a brawl with someone who cares more about inflicting pain than the overall outcome of the contest can be dangerous.

And I have been on the other side of this scenario thousands of times, which is a nightmare!

"He's too quick."

"I can't jump with this guy."

"Man, I just can't stop him!"

There is also something special about fighting the fight regardless of the odds—even when you're outmatched. Building resiliency leads to more strength, toughness, and continuous improvement. We get better when we compete against the best. This can also force us to get more innovative when adversity comes. When the challenge is extreme, we get to experiment and do something different to determine the most likely path toward victory. What an amazing challenge—perhaps something like what you're currently experiencing.

Don't let people less talented than you outwork you, get in your head, and/or bring you down to their level by reducing the game to a rock fight!

But if you need to reduce the game to a rock fight, don't be afraid to take an unconventional path.

Lies! Lies! Lies!

"The worst lies are the lies we tell ourselves."

— Richard Bach

We lie to ourselves (which can often be damaging).

And the lies others tell us, we frequently believe.

Regardless of whether these lies are true, they become truth—manifesting reality.

This includes the illusion that your value is a product of your statistics. Not true!

Another common lie is that "this" performance and my sport reflect my identity. These lies can be delivered to you by the media, family members, friends, and by that gray matter in between our ears.

Several other lies often show up when transitioning into life away from the game. You're new to this work world and you need to start at the bottom and pay your dues. As you learned while competing, paying your dues with hard work and the right habits can drive success. But don't fool yourself into thinking the attributes that served you during competition do not translate into success during the next phase of your life. Imagine you get to hire someone, and a potential candidate has experience in one of these areas:

- Performing under pressure
- Making good decisions
- Working in a team environment
- Demonstrating discipline
- Handling conflict
- Leveraging resources

These qualities and experiences that you have executed countless times are highly coveted in the marketplace. Think about how inferior a person without athletic experience might feel. That person comes to the table with less of a head start.

So, when we lie, we must do so strategically and use our imagination.

"You may say I'm a dreamer
But I'm not the only one
I hope someday you'll join us
And the world will live as one"
— John Lennon

"… But it was just my imagination
Runnin' away with me
It was just my imagination
Runnin' away with me"
— The Temptations

The power of imagination is real, and it enables us to change the narrative:

Imagine how you would show up and perform without limiting beliefs in your way. Imagine becoming "who you're supposed to be" as opposed to chasing someone else's version of what your success and happiness should look like.

Here's an example of how lying the right way can serve us. We can lean into a time when we dominated and circulate these thoughts to create a new reality. Or we can simply make stuff up and lie to ourselves about the time we crossed over Michael Jordan. Lying to ourselves to elevate our mindset can serve us and drive the intended outcome. Our thoughts become emotions, which lead to action. This means we need to constantly replay our mental highlight reels. We must tell ourselves the right story!

Johnnie LeMaster was a baseball player who played in the major leagues for over ten years. Although his career batting average of .222 didn't set the world on fire, he did something interesting to change the narrative of what he was hearing. He replaced "LeMaster" on the back of his uniform with a new name—"Boo!"

Just like that, the boos of disgust were converted into the entire stadium wildly cheering and chanting for Johnnie!

No one has the power to determine your value unless you surrender that power. Tell yourself stories that will move you closer to your desired outcome, not further away from your vision.

Damn, I wish I had one more in me!

> "I miss the game - I miss it a lot."
>
> — Joe Montana

Skills erode, but the emotions and memories of competing are everlasting. In some ways, they get stronger over time.

Even when reflecting on the most intense practices when your coach, trainer, or torture chamber expert took the pain to an unrealistic level, nostalgic thoughts of "Those were some pretty good times!" surface.

It's like when you were hanging on for dear life in college, or you were pursuing your path toward success. During these times, you were probably feeding your face with an abundance of nutritious ramen noodles (processed with 2,500 grams of sodium), and similar thoughts of "Those were some pretty good times" invaded your headspace.

A long time ago, I played with a team that traveled to Honolulu for a tournament. We were scheduled to compete against several schools, including BYU and Pacific University. We did a walk-around at the arena where the games would take place, and even though the public was not present (we hadn't even had our practice sessions yet), the space was electric and extremely cool. As thoughts of "Stay calm, relax, focus" showed up in my head, I heard one of our coaches say, "Damn, I wish I had one more game in me!"

And although he did not have one more game in him, that moment served as a reminder. Regardless of how long you have played or at what level, we always want one more!

And in some ways, we believe we can summon the power and play one more game. And by the way, I can still shoot. The ball never goes in, but I can still physically shoot the basketball!

You don't need to delete those life-changing memories, but there needs to be a balance. If most of your time is spent looking in the rearview mirror as opposed to what's next, a healthy balance has yet to be achieved. It's okay to be emotionally attached to the game, practices, and locker room, but we've got to be sure that most of our time is invested in the "now what?" zone. What was so exciting about competition in those days that made me feel alive? How can I replicate that feeling and pursue my next adventure with enthusiasm and optimism? What am I most passionate about? Who do I need to surround myself with to achieve that, and what specific action do I need to take that will allow that vision to come to fruition?

You've got at least one more game left in you. You've got a lot left in the tank—but you must play differently and even smarter.

Retaliation

"Smile, people will wonder what you're up to."

— Sean Keogh

Shout out to Junior Giscombe and his hit from the early eighties, entitled, *"Mama Used to Say,"* (mercifully you cannot hear me sing this, but here is a small sample of the lyrics):

And mama used to say
"Take your time young man"
And mama used to say
"Don't you rush to get old"
And mama used to say
"Take it in your stride"
And mama used to say
"Live your life"

Let's stick with the line "Take your time young man."

When stuff happens while competing athletically or in business and life, what are you going to do about it? When are you going to do it?

Exhibit A

You just received a cheap shot while battling under the boards. Now, what are you going to do? Regardless of the sport, have you ever been here? And have you ever been here and retaliated immediately? How did that turn out for you? I can tell you that, for me, I retaliated within three seconds and was given a technical foul. So, I lost by receiving a cheap shot. I lost again by getting into foul trouble, and I lost yet again because I put my team in a situation that reduced our chances of winning.

What is a better play?

I'm not letting you off the hook by retaliating immediately. Although I might do something horrible to you, I'd much rather have you suffer with the uncertainty of when it is going to happen.

Take your time, young men and young women (and even those who are not so young—like me!)

Understand the when and how of responding to people in your personal and professional circles who try to push your buttons.

Confidence, transition, and takeaways

"Work ethic eliminates fear. If you put forth the work, then what are you fearing?"

— Michael Jordan

One of the best feelings on earth is knowing that you put in the work and are prepared physically and mentally. While competing, this creates a mindset of "If I'm tired, this guy must be ready to pass out!"—which generates some serious confidence!

But if you haven't put in the work and you are not ready, you might try lying to yourself to convince yourself that you're ready for the moment. Good luck with that!

Roy Firestone once had an interview show called *Up Close*. In 1984, he interviewed college head basketball coach, Jim Valvano, who shared some powerful insight concerning athletes and transitioning away from the game.

"The cheering is going to stop, and you've got to be prepared for that!"

He went on to describe that the seventeen-year-old who previously played in front of millions, will no longer experience a daily and enthusiastic introduction:

"At left desk—Brian Wood!"

It's not about what happens, but what you do about it. This is a complicated and exciting journey you're experiencing. There is no "one-size-fits-all" solution—the game plan must be personal, unique, and customized. Here are a few parting reminders of some dynamics that can be baked into your action plan.

Reminders

- You are not on an island. Don't fight this alone. While you were competing, you had a team (teammates, coaches, and trainers). Make sure you draft the right team now to support your next chapter of greatness!

- Once your playing days are over, showing up at a staff meeting and challenging the room with "I'm going to post you up and physically destroy you" hardly ever ends well. But you can use intensity as a strength and not a liability.
- Deliberate practice, drills, hydration, nutrition, weightlifting, and all other habits that formerly served your athletic vision can be implemented in a way that supports your next adventure. This might involve replacing sprints with daily reading and/or journaling. But the act of deliberately planning your day and learning the life playbook will speed up your path toward success away from the game.
- Serve others. One of the best strategies that can cultivate a winning mindset is seeking opportunities to help others. This can be a random act of kindness or something more involved. Serving others while we figure things out often moves us away from a victim mindset toward one of gratitude and possibilities.
- Ask for support. If I can do something to support your world and your journey toward greatness—I got you!

Leverage your crazy as needed but use it as your secret weapon. You have the power to tap into the intensity that drove results while competing. Call it in from the bullpen, but don't allow others to use this power against you.

ABOUT BRIAN

Brian Wood is a highly sought-after executive coach and President of MARS Coaching. With thirty years of corporate experience and a background as an athlete, certified player agent (NBA, WNBA, and FIBA), and certified professional success coach, Brian offers clients a unique perspective and guidance toward the next level of achievement.

Brian is passionate about helping leaders find their passion and leverage their gifts to achieve their definition of success. His expertise in continuous personal and professional growth, including organizational development, training, and gamification, has earned him recognition as a Professional Certified Coach (PCC) by the International Coaching Federation (ICF).

Brian's extensive experience includes providing confidential, professional, and executive coaching, virtual and in-person facilitation, and all aspects of leadership development training and organizational development needs. He has worked with major corporations, professional sports organizations, and municipalities to achieve their goals and reach their full potential.

Furthermore, Brian is a Board Member with Big Brothers Big Sisters of Central Arizona, a Development Dimensions

International (DDI) Certified Facilitator, a Foundation Board Member at William Paterson University, Wayne, NJ, and an Advisory Board Member for the College of Arts, Humanities, and Social Sciences at William Paterson University.

With his proven track record of success, Brian is an executive coach with the American Express Leadership Academy hosted by the Arizona State University Lodestar Center for Philanthropy and nonprofit innovation and a small group facilitator with the T4 Leadership Academy at ASU. He is also a Success Coach with the Humanitarian Coaching Network and a Transition Coach with Athletes Soul.

Brian earned his BA in Communications from William Paterson University and his MBA in 2014 from the University of Phoenix. If you are looking to take your leadership and personal development to the next level, Brian is the coach you need.

https://www.linkedin.com/in/brianwoodmba/
https://www.instagram.com/woodmarscoach/
https://www.facebook.com/MarsCoaching
https://twitter.com/woodmarscoach

CONCLUSION

Throughout this book, you have delved into the athletic journeys of several former athletes from various sports and countries. These stories were riddled with setbacks and challenges, such as injuries, failures, unfulfilled dreams, and even traumatic experiences. Regardless of their level and results, these athletes encountered an immense amount of pain and obstacles.

This is the harsh reality of elite sport: it is arduous, unpredictable, and often inequitable. However, as these athletes reflect on their experiences, it is clear that these experiences have had a significant impact on their lives and have helped shape their personalities and character.

Retirement represents the ultimate challenge at the end of an athlete's career. It is yet another obstacle to overcome, and perhaps the most challenging one. For some athletes, it took years to recover from their transition away from sport. Nevertheless, instead of turning their backs on their sport, our authors all acknowledge the importance of their athletic experience in their lives, and how, even years later, it remains at the core of who they are.

In addition to sport, it is the life lessons learned through sports that unite all of these individuals. Through their athletic careers, they discovered what they were truly made of. They learned to push their physical and mental limits, persevered despite repeated failures, and understood the significance of consistency and commitment. They didn't learn these skills through books, but through firsthand experience.

The struggles these athletes faced were matched by intense moments of joy and success. These former athletes also appreciate the opportunity to meet and work with others from diverse backgrounds. Teamwork and the ability to collaborate with others are seen as tremendous benefits of being an athlete. Sport is the ultimate melting pot, providing an opportunity for personal growth and, at times, a source of immense satisfaction.

Transformed by their experiences, they have all found a way to give back to their sport or the athletic community. Each author, in their unique way, shares their personal experiences and skills with current athletes. In the second part of this book, several of them share their advice and systems for dealing with athletic retirement and how to transition more confidently. Because no two transitions are alike, offering multiple ways to cope with this period of uncertainty is beneficial.

To athletes and former athletes who read this book, we hope it has provided comfort, insight, and advice to help you understand your own athletic retirement and transition experience. If you would like to learn more about Athletes Soul and its services, and how we can support you, please visit our website at www.athletessoul.org.

ACKNOWLEDGEMENTS

We would like to thank all co-authors for sharing their stories and insights and for their support to retiring athletes. With the donations received from our co-authors, we were able to provide individual transition coaching to ten athletes for three months.

We also want to extend a very special thank you to Taj Dashaun, who is a longtime supporter of Athletes Soul and has helped us make this book a reality.

ABOUT ATHLETES SOUL

A thletes Soul is a non-profit organization funded and run by former athletes. The organization's mission is to support athletes as they transition away from sport, raise awareness about the challenges of athletic retirement, and empower athletes to develop beyond sport.

We offer educational resources, transition and career coaching, and networking opportunities to support athletes before, during, and after they retire from sports. Our services are available to athletes from all sports and levels, and at no cost to the athletes. For more information about Athletes Soul, visit www.athletessoul.org.

To enquire about our services and support: www.athletessoul.org/services

To support Athletes Soul's efforts: www.athletessoul.org/donations

Made in the USA
Middletown, DE
23 January 2024

48015192R10126